T0360723

Cambridge Elements ≡

Elements in Corporate Governance
edited by
Thomas Clarke
UTS Business School, University of Technology Sydney

THE RHETORIC AND REALITY OF SHAREHOLDER DEMOCRACY AND HEDGE-FUND ACTIVISM

Jang-Sup Shin
National University of Singapore

CAMBRIDGE
UNIVERSITY PRESS

CAMBRIDGE
UNIVERSITY PRESS

Shaftesbury Road, Cambridge CB2 8EA, United Kingdom

One Liberty Plaza, 20th Floor, New York, NY 10006, USA

477 Williamstown Road, Port Melbourne, VIC 3207, Australia

314–321, 3rd Floor, Plot 3, Splendor Forum, Jasola District Centre,
New Delhi – 110025, India

103 Penang Road, #05–06/07, Visioncrest Commercial, Singapore 238467

Cambridge University Press is part of Cambridge University Press & Assessment,
a department of the University of Cambridge.

We share the University's mission to contribute to society through the pursuit of
education, learning and research at the highest international levels of excellence.

www.cambridge.org
Information on this title: www.cambridge.org/9781009576413

DOI: 10.1017/9781009576444

First published 2024

A catalogue record for this publication is available from the British Library.

ISBN 978-1-009-57641-3 Hardback
ISBN 978-1-009-57643-7 Paperback
ISSN 2515-7175 (online)
ISSN 2515-7167 (print)

The Rhetoric and Reality of Shareholder Democracy and Hedge-Fund Activism

Elements in Corporate Governance

DOI: 10.1017/9781009576444
First published online: November 2024

Jang-Sup Shin
National University of Singapore

Author for correspondence: Jang-Sup Shin, ecssjs@nus.edu.sg

Abstract: This Element investigates the historical and systemic roots of hedge-fund activism. It argues that the spirit of the New Deal financial regulations was subverted in the 1980s and 1990s in the name of shareholder democracy and opened the door for the rise of hedge-fund activism. It analyzes the effects of regulatory reforms including the introduction of compulsory voting by institutional investors, proxy-voting rule changes that greatly facilitated aggregation of the proxy votes of institutional investors, and rules that allow hedge funds to draw effectively limitless alternative investments from institutional investors. This Element also evaluates the recent empirical research on hedge-fund activism and explains why shareholder activism has gone awry. It argues that the regulatory changes created a large vacuum in the arena of corporate voting that hedge-fund activists can effectively exploit for their own profits. It concludes with policy proposals for rebuilding the proxy-voting and engagement system.

Keywords: shareholder democracy, hedge-fund activism, proxy rules, value creation and extraction, proxy advisory firms

ISBNs: 9781009576413 (HB), 9781009576437 (PB), 9781009576444 (OC)
ISSNs: 2515-7175 (online), 2515-7167 (print)

Contents

1 Introduction

The value-extracting power of hedge-fund activists is hardly comprehensible to casual observers. They are mere "minority shareholders." Yet they exert enormous influence over corporations, often forcing them to undertake fundamental restructuring and to increase stock buybacks and dividends substantially. For instance, Third Point Management and Trian Fund Management, holding only 2 percent of the outstanding stock of Dow Chemical and Du Pont, respectively, engineered a merger-and-split of America's top two chemical giants at the end of 2015, resulting in massive layoffs and closure of DuPont's central research lab, the first industrial science lab in the United States.[1] Carl Icahn, after acquiring about 1 percent of Apple's stock in 2013, pressed the most valuable company at the time to repurchase a record-breaking $80 billion of its outstanding stock in 2014–2015 and took $2 billion of profit for himself when he sold his entire stake in 2016.[2]

Elliot Management, which had already attracted wide attention as a "vulture fund" by enforcing full payment of junk bonds issued by poor countries in Africa and Latin America through litigation and other measures, purchased about 0.5 percent of the outstanding stock of Samsung Electronics in early fiscal 2016. It then demanded that the largest electronics company in the world by revenue split itself into a holding company and an operating company while radically increasing "shareholder-friendly" measures by paying out special dividends of about $26 billion (KRW30 trillion). This hedge-fund attack led the company to embark on about $8 billion (KRW9.4 trillion) of additional stock buybacks on top of about $9.9 billion (KRW11.3 trillion) of stock buybacks it had been doing over the previous year, apparently as "compensation" for its rejection of Elliott's demand to split the company and pay a special dividend.[3] It is now increasingly difficult to find incidents in which management goes against hedge-fund activists' proposals outright and risks proceeding to a proxy voting showdown in shareholder meetings. As Steven D. Solomon (2015) commented, "companies, frankly, are scared" and "[their] mantra . . . is to settle with hedge funds before it gets to a fight over the control of a company."

This book explains why and how hedge-fund activists have acquired power disproportionate to their actual shareholding and discusses its implications for government policy and corporate management. Hedge-fund activists are descendants of the corporate raiders whose junk-bond-fueled attacks on US businesses in the 1980s were at the center of what became known as the "deal decade." With the collapse of the junk bond market in the late 1980s, corporate

---

[1] Gandel (2015); Team (2016); Traeger (2018).   [2] Lazonick et al. (2016).
[3] Merced (2016); Mirae Asset (2017); Kolhatkar (2018).

raiders reinvented themselves as "hedge-fund activists."[4] Both corporate raiders and hedge-fund activists exploit their positions as shareholders to extract value from companies. However, hedge-fund activists differ from their predecessors in that they extract value while remaining minority shareholders, whereas corporate raiders do so by becoming (or threatening to become) majority shareholders.

This book argues that the power of these "minority-shareholding corporate raiders" derives from misguided regulatory "reforms" carried out in the 1980s and 1990s in the name of "shareholder democracy." It points out that shareholder democracy began in the early twentieth century as a political rhetoric to build a more cohesive society by making citizens own shares of corporations and becoming sympathizers of capitalist development. At the time, there was no economic rhetoric. Advocates of shareholder democracy made it clear that it had nothing to do with improving the economic efficiency of corporations and were not interested in making public shareholders influence management decisions. Shareholder democracy remained a political rhetoric, not an economic one, for nearly a half-century until the 1980s (Section 2).

From the 1980s, shareholder democracy began to transform into an economic rhetoric with the rise of shareholder activism. Section 3 delineates how this rhetoric emerged and became broadly accepted by the public and policymakers, and how it was captured by hedge-fund activists for their profits. It deals with various regulatory changes toward encouraging shareholder activism, including the introduction of compulsory voting by institutional shareholders, proxy-voting rule changes that greatly facilitated hedge-fund activists' aggregation of the proxy votes of institutional investors, and allowing hedge funds to draw unlimited funds from institutional shareholders to conduct their attacks on target corporations. It also discusses the rapid growth of institutional shareholding, and the growing acceptance of agency theory and the maximizing shareholder value (AT-MSV) view that underpinned those regulatory changes.

Because of the big discrepancy between the rhetoric and reality of shareholder democracy, shareholder activism failed to achieve its intended objectives. Section 4 investigates empirical evidence of institutional activism and

---

[4] Corporate raiders in fact bifurcated into hedge-fund activists and private-equity funds. In the latter, traditional methods of corporate raiding by becoming majority shareholders continued to be practiced although the conventional term, "hostile takeover," gave way to simple "takeover" as hostile takeover activities were established as a norm in the corporate and financial world. This book only focuses on the transformation of corporate raiders into hedge-fund activists. I also prefer using "hedge-fund activists" to "activist hedge funds" because some prominent activists like Carl Icahn engage in activism with their own companies without setting up funds although most of those activists are funds.

hedge-fund activism. It emphasizes that it was already evident to researchers by the early 2010s that institutional activism failed and those who were sympathetic to shareholder activism shifted their focus to hedge-fund activism. The section critically examines the research that purportedly shows the positive effects of hedge-fund activism and points out that hedge-fund activism also failed to achieve economic improvement of corporations and is more likely to have resulted in "predatory value extraction."

Section 5 delves into the question of why shareholder activism has gone astray. More than anything else, it was because its economic rhetoric is simply a rhetoric not supported by economic reality. The section explains this detachment of rhetoric from economic reality by the distinction between value creation and value extraction. It also stresses that contrary to shareholder activists' expectation that institutional shareholders would develop capabilities to involve themselves in the value creation process of corporations, they evolved into entities that are less capable of and less interested in corporate affairs because of the rapid growth of index funds. Combined with the dominance of index funds among institutional shareholders, the regulatory changes in the 1980s and 1990s such as imposing voting as a fiduciary duty of institutional shareholders and allowing free communication and engagement between shareholders and corporate management created a large vacuum in the arena of corporate voting that hedge-fund activists can effectively exploit for their own profit. The book concludes with suggestions for rebuilding the shareholder voting and engagement system to encourage the long-term value creation of corporations (Section 6).

2 The Rhetoric and Reality of Shareholder Democracy

In understanding shareholder democracy and the rise of hedge-fund activism in the US, it is crucial to recognize that shareholder democracy started in the early twentieth century as a political project for social cohesion, not as an economic project with economic rationales to support it. As a political project, it was premised on retail shareholders who had political rights in society through voting in elections and other forms of political participation. Institutional shareholders, not having such political rights, were not part of the movement for shareholder democracy. They were instead placed under heavy regulations because regulators then regarded them mainly as potential market manipulators. The early promoters of shareholder democracy also took shareholder passivity for granted, even for retail shareholders. The economic inclusion of retail shareholders was confined to sharing the passive economic benefits of holding shares in the form of receiving dividends and realizing capital gains. This passivity of retail shareholders in the earlier days differed from the current-day shareholder democracy led by the activism of institutional shareholders.

2.1 The Political Origin of Shareholder Democracy in the Early Twentieth Century

When the US public stock market took shape in the early twentieth century, those who came to own public shares sold by retiring founder-shareholders were mostly retail shareholders – that is, individual households. They were fundamentally passive investors. Each holding a minuscule percentage of a corporation's shares outstanding, they had no ability or incentive to engage with corporate management. They were only concerned with monetary rights attached to the stocks they owned, such as entitlements to dividends and capital gains. Their general willingness to leave control to managers stemmed in part from the prior revenue-generating successes of those corporations and partly from the trust the shareholders had in financial intermediaries who had persuaded them to buy those corporate stocks. More fundamentally, being passive was a rational choice for these retail shareholders because the shares they held were liquid so that they could sell them on the stock market at any time, a maneuver that became known as "the Wall Street Walk." They would not have purchased the shares in the beginning had they been obliged to be active and commit time and effort to oversee corporate management.[5]

The movement for shareholder democracy progressed with the emergence of these retail shareholders. Promoters of shareholder democracy envisioned a more cohesive society where mass workers would turn into mass shareholders supporting corporations and capitalism. John Bates Clark, a neoclassical economist, expected at the turn of the century that the share ownership by workers would "blur, or perhaps disappear … the old line of demarcation between the capitalist class and the laboring class," and argued that "[t]he socialist is not the only man who can have beatific visions."[6] This vision continued into the 1920s. John Raskob, a financier and businessman who played a crucial role in the expansion of Du Pont and General Motors, for instance, famously stated, "Everybody ought to be rich," when he laid out proposals for working- and middle-class wealth building in a 1929 article in *Ladies Home Journal*.[7]

---

[5] Lazonick and O'Sullivan (2000).   [6] Quoted in Ott (2011, p. 25).

[7] Crowther (1929), Hagley Museum and Library. https://findingaids.hagley.org/xtf/view?docId=ead/0473.xml (accessed August 17, 2021). Ott (2011) similarly points out that political and economic leaders at the time hoped that mass share-ownership of corporations would "shore up the propertied foundations of citizenship, preserve economic mobility and autonomy, enhance national prosperity, and make corporations accord with the will of the people." (p. 4).

In the same context, Julia Ott (2011) states in *When Wall Street Met Main Street: The Quest for Investors' Democracy*, the primary concern of "intellectual, political, corporate, and financial leaders who embarked on a quest for mass investment" was how to build a stable and prosperous political system in the face of not only public distrust of "corporate power and accountability" but also of political challenges of internal integration from "mounting economic inequality, surging immigration, ethnic diversity, Jim Crow segregation, and women's demands for suffrage [that] sparked fundamental debates about citizenship." They hoped that "[m]ass investment could shore up the propertied foundations of citizenship, preserve economic mobility and autonomy, enhance national prosperity, and make corporations accord with the will of the people" (p. 4).

While promoting shareholder democracy as a political project, they made it clear that they did not think of it as being related to raising capital. According to Ott, they "did not view mass investment as a particularly efficient or profitable means of raising capital," and the "[c]orporate need for capital did not call forth popular demand for financial securities spontaneously."[8] In other words, the promoters of shareholder democracy did not employ an economic rhetoric that would improve the economic efficiency of corporations or the economy. William Lazonick and Mary O'Sullivan point out in the same context: "The stock market [at the time] did not serve as a source of funds for long-term business investment. When an enterprise went public, the stock market was the instrument for the separation of stock ownership from strategic control over internally generated corporate revenues."[9]

Because the promotion of shareholder democracy was a political project, institutional shareholders were not included in the movement because they were fiduciaries, not citizens who had political rights of representation. Institutional shareholders, such as mutual funds, were only beginning to emerge and held only about 5 percent of the US equity market capitalization by 1929.[10] They were considered merely money managers who functioned to diversify investments, thereby raising yields on portfolio investments while managing risks, an option not available to most retail shareholders.

This diversifying function of institutional shareholders had been well established from the days of the first collective investment trusts that emerged in Scotland and the UK in the latter half of the nineteenth century. For instance, the stated goal of the Foreign and Colonial Government Investment Trust established in 1868 was "to give the investor of moderate means the same advantages as the large capitalist in diminishing the risk of investing in Foreign and

---

[8] Ott (2011, p. 4).   [9] Lazonick and O'Sullivan (2000, p. 112).
[10] McGrattan and Prescott (2004), cited in Coates (2018, p. 8).

Colonial Government Stocks, by spreading the investment over a number of different stocks."[11]

2.2 New Deal Financial Regulations of Institutional Shareholders

In line with the overall spirit of shareholder democracy in those days, New Deal financial regulations established in the 1930s emphasized the passivity of public shareholders and specifically discouraged institutional activism. As a policy response to the turmoil of the 1929 New York Stock Exchange crash and the subsequent collapse of economic activity, the Securities Act of 1933 and the Securities Exchange Act of 1934 sought to regulate financial markets.[12] A few years later, Congress passed the Investment Company Act of 1940, which regulated institutional shareholders.[13]

These New Deal regulations embodied three enduring principles that would guide the relationship between shareholders and companies: (1) the prohibition of fraud and deceit, including profiting from insider information; (2) regulating any shareholders acting as a group and prohibiting the formation of investors' cartels; and (3) encouraging institutional shareholders to diversify their portfolios and discouraging them from exerting influence over management.

Under the first principle, the regulations required public companies to make regular, accurate, and timely public disclosures of financial information to shareholders[14] and barred shareholders and managers from misappropriating corporate resources and profiting from insider information.[15] They specifically prohibited "fraudulent ... manipulative [and] deceptive conduct."[16] To deter insider trading, they required those who were deemed insiders, whether manager-owners or investors, to disclose "all the information prior to trading."[17]

---

[11] Coates (2018, p. 7).

[12] Securities Exchange Act (1933; 15 U.S.C. §§ 77a-77mm) ("1933 Act" henceforth); Securities Exchange Act (1934; 15 U.S.C. § 78a-78jj) ("1934 Act" henceforce). The 1933 Act is the first major federal legislation to regulate the offer and sale of securities. It is based upon a philosophy of disclosure, meaning that the goal of the law is to require issuers to fully disclose all material information that a reasonable shareholder would need in order to make up his or her mind about the potential investment. The 1934 Act forms the basis of regulation of the financial markets and their participants. While the 1933 Act is about the primary market, The 1934 Act regulates the secondary market. It also established the Securities and Exchange Commission (SEC).

[13] Investment Company Act (1940; 15 U.S.C. §§ 80a-1–80a-64) ("1940 Act" henceforth). The 1940 Act specifically regulates investment companies, including mutual funds, and seeks to protect the public primarily by requiring disclosure of material details about each investment company.

[14] 1934 Act, § 13(a) (l).　　[15] 1934 Act, § 10b, 17 C.F.R. § 240.10b-5.

[16] 1934 Act, §§ 9, 10(b), 15(c), 15 U.S.C §§ 78i(a), 78j(b), 78o(c). See also Blair (1995); Roe (1990).

[17] 1934 Act, § § 10b-5(c), 16(a), 15 U.S.C 78p(a); Blair (1995, p. 51).

In addition, the regulations outlined that, should insiders profit by buying a company's securities and selling them within six months or vice versa, they "are recoverable by the issuer [the company]."[18]

Under the second principle, the formation of a voting group by investors was heavily regulated as establishing an investor cartel. If the combined shares of a group of investors exceeded 10 percent of the company's stock, its members were subject to the same regulations as insiders.[19] Furthermore, communications between investors were subject to strict oversight to prevent the development of such a group. If a group is to be formed, its prospective members should communicate with each other. The regulations, therefore, judged the communication as a proxy solicitation and made it necessary to file it by providing the information specified in Schedule 14A of the 1934 Act.[20] Blair (1995), therefore, points out that the regulations made it "difficult for shareholders to communicate with each other at all ... without the approval and support of management" (p. 71).

Under the third principle, institutional shareholders were encouraged to diversify their portfolios and discouraged from seeking to control management. The 1934 Pecora Report, the product of a Senate securities investigation, explicitly walled institutional shareholders off from management, making it clear that mutual funds were only allowed to engage in investment activities.[21] This principle was also embodied in the Tax Code of 1936: "another safeguard ... is to prevent an investment trust or investment corporation [from] being set up to obtain control of some corporation and to manipulate its affairs."[22] In testimony regarding the enactment of the Investment Company Act of 1940, a high-ranking SEC official asserted that "a mutual fund's *only* positive function was to provide diversification; any extension risked thievery."[23]

This regulation clearly separating management from institutional shareholders answered in part the need to remove the potential for conflicts of interest: If institutional shareholders were allowed to control corporations, they would tend to utilize their position for their own profit at the expense of other shareholders. More importantly, behind the regulation was a clear understanding that corporate managers and institutional shareholders serve different functions: While the former seeks to create value in corporations by producing high-quality and low-cost goods and services, the latter helps individuals extract

---

[18] 1934 Act, § 16(b), 15 U.S.C. § 78p(b); Blair (1995, p. 51).

[19] *See* 1940 Act, §§ 2(a)(2)-(3), 17(a)-(b), 15 U.S.C. §§ 80a-2(a)(2)-(3), 80a-17(a)-(b).

[20] *See* 17 C.F.R. § 240.14a-l(k) (2021); SEC Release No. 3347 (December 18, 1942); 17 C.F.R. § 240.14a-2b(1) & 3(a) (2021); Roe (1990, p. 17).

[21] U.S. Senate Committee of Banking and Currency (2009); Roe (1991). For details on the Pecora Report, see Perino (2010).

[22] Roe (1991, p. 1483).   [23] Roe (1991, p. 1488). The emphasis is original.

value from corporations by leveraging size and diversification of corporate shareholding.[24] The mutual fund industry did not oppose the government in imposing the regulations at the time because they legitimized the industry in the eyes of the public.[25]

These three principles had been well enough established and went unchallenged until the 1980s. As recently as 1974, Congress upheld the same principles when it introduced the Employee Retirement Income Security Act (ERISA), a policy response to the growing need to regulate pensions. First, ERISA's rules prevented self-dealing behavior on the part of employers and fund managers.[26] Second, they discouraged pension funds from taking excessive risks and encouraged them to diversify investment portfolios broadly.[27] Third, they urged pension funds to refrain from exercising control over companies in their portfolio.[28] In this context, Peter Drucker, one of the earliest thinkers who envisaged the coming of the Pension Fund Revolution, pointed out that pension funds "have no business trying to 'manage' ... To sit on a board of directors ... and accept the obligations of board membership, is incompatible with duties as 'trustees' ... which have been sharply and strictly defined in the Pension Fund Reform Act of 1974 [ERISA]."[29]

3 The Progression of Shareholder Activism and the Rise of Hedge-Fund Activism

Beginning in the 1980s, however, the three principles established during the New Deal era increasingly came under assault. It became easier for shareholders to form de facto voting groups, seriously impairing the second principle. The loosening of regulations on shareholders' communication and concerted actions was legitimatized by the new credos of "corporate citizenship" and "relational investing" that encouraged the active participation of institutional shareholders,[30] moving drastically away from the third principle. The first principle did not change much for public shareholders, but the adoption of SEC Rule 10b-18 in 1982, which allowed corporate executives to manipulate stock prices through stock buybacks, damaged the first principle and opened room for activist shareholders' demand for stock buybacks.[31]

---

[24] On value creation by business corporation and value extraction through the stock market, refer to Section 5.1. Also see Lazonick and Shin (2020, pp. 14–40, 41–89).

[25] Roe (1991, p. 1489).

[26] 29 U.S.C. § 1104(a)(1)(A)(i); 29 U.S.C § 1101; Blair (1995, p. 157).

[27] 29 U.S.C. § 1104(a)(1)(C); Blair (1995, p. 157).

[28] 29 U.S.C. § 1144(b)(2)(B); Blair (1995, p. 157).   [29] Drucker (1976, p. 63).

[30] For the understanding of these terms, see Section 3.1.

[31] On the SEC Rule 10b-18 in 1982 and its impacts, refer to Lazonick (2014a, 2019); Lazonick and Shin (2020).

There were various groups of activists who pursued changes in the relationship between public shareholders and corporations. Some of them wanted to obtain what they considered public benefits by doing so. At the same time, there were groups of market players, including corporate raiders, who did not hide their raw intention of profiting from the process of "reforming" corporations. Despite their differences in motives and mode of action, those activists formed a common front under the banner of shareholder democracy against corporate managers whom they accused of building their fiefdoms by investing in wasteful projects while ignoring the interests of public shareholders. They were also common in finding ways to leverage the rapidly growing voting power of institutional shareholders. Regulatory authorities, such as the SEC, the DOL, and the Department of Treasury, started to side with the activists. These actions were also legitimized by the growing acceptance of agency theory and the "maximizing shareholder value" (AT-MSV) view, which asserted that corporate managers are agents of shareholders, and their purpose is to maximize shareholder value.[32] This section discusses how they succeeded in bringing about significant changes in the traditional New Deal financial regulations.[33] The upshot of the regulatory changes is presented in Figure 1.

3.1 The Growing Voting Power of Institutional Shareholders

The share ownership structure of US corporations is conventionally characterized as "dispersed ownership." Since 1932, when Adolf Berle and Gardiner Means offered this classic characterization and pointed out the "separation of ownership and control" as its result, it has been the starting point of the debate on corporate governance and economic performance.[34] Undoubtedly, the shareholding of major corporations in the United States is still dispersed compared with those in other countries. However, the characteristics of the dispersion have undergone qualitative changes. If the classic dispersion saw shares in the hands of retail investors who were the actual owners of the shares, the prominent feature of the current-day dispersion is that shares are in the hands of institutional shareholders, fiduciaries of the savers who are the shares' ultimate owners.

This institutionalization of shareholding progressed through the latter half of the twentieth century and has continued in the twenty-first century. As shown in Figure 2, the institutional shareholding of US public stocks was at only 7.2 percent

---

[32] Refer to Sections 3.5 and 5.1 for details on agency theory and the MSV view.
[33] On the evolution of corporate governance discourse, refer to Cheffins (2013); Blair (1995); Veasey (1993).
[34] Berle and Means (1932). For criticisms of this kind of characterization, refer to Pichhadze (2010, 2012). Also, refer to Section 5.1 for understanding the term as the "dispersion of corporate control" rather than the "separation of ownership and control."

The New Deal Financial Regulations in the 1930s

• Establishing the principle of separation
between public shareholders and corporate management

ERISA Regulation in 1974

• Continuation of the New Deal principles

Formalizing Institutional Activism in 1985-86

• Establishment of Council of Institutional Investors (CII) (1985)

• Establishment of Institutional Shareholder Services (ISS) (1985)

• Launch of United Shareholder Association (USA) (1986)

Avon Letter and DOL-DOF Directives in 1988-9

• Compulsory voting for pension funds

SEC Proxy Rule Change in 1992

• Allowing *de facto* investor cartels

• Unlimited freedom of "communication and engagement"

NSMIA on Hedge Funds in 1996

• Allowing unlimited "alternative investment" in hedge funds

SEC Final Rule on Proxy Voting in 2003

• Compulsory voting for mutual funds and other investment advisers

---

Figure 1 Changes in regulations on the relation between institutional
shareholders and corporations

in 1950 but continued to increase to 40.0 percent in 1980 and 59.8 percent in 2020. In Figure 2, drawn from the Federal Reserve dataset, hedge funds and private-equity funds are classified as "households," not as "institutional shareholders," despite the fact that most of them function as institutions by pooling and managing

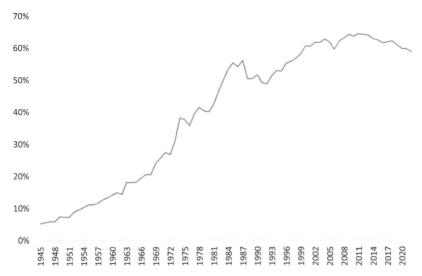

Figure 2 The growth of institutional shareholding in the United States

Source: Estimated from Z.1 Statistical Release of Federal Reserve Board (The Federal Reserve Board website, www.federalreserve.gov/datadownload/Download.aspx?rel= Z1&series=75cf7aa5c5495b9ba5194795df5ee426&from=01/01/1945&to=12/31/2023 &lastObs=&filetype=spreadsheetml&label=include&layout=seriesrow (Accessed on July 30, 2023)).

other people's money.[35] If one includes hedge funds and private-equity funds in institutional shareholders, the actual institutional shareholding percentages would be substantially higher than what Figure 2 shows. For instance, *Pensions & Investment* estimated institutional holding as 80.3 percent of the market value of the S&P 500 index and 78.1 percent of the US broad-market Russell 3000 index in 2017, while the Fed data indicate the institutional share as 61.9 percent.[36]

3.2 Imposing Compulsory Voting on Institutional Shareholders: Robert Monks and ISS

In transforming institutional shareholders into activists, Robert Monks, who described himself as "an entrepreneur of the idea of corporate governance,"[37] was the principal ideologue, administrator, and businessman, almost single-handedly making proxy voting a fiduciary duty of institutional shareholders

---

[35] 'Non-profit organizations such as university endowment funds are also not included here. The apparent slowdown of the growth in institutional shareholding after 2016 in Figure 2 has to do with the boom of private equities, hedge funds, endowment funds, and sovereign wealth funds, which are not classified as institutions in Fed's shareholding dataset.

[36] "80% of Equity Market Cap Held by Institutions," *Pension & Investments* (April 25, 2017), www.pionline.com/article/20170425/INTERACTIVE/170429926/80-of-equity-market-cap-held-by-institutions (Accessed on July 20, 2020).

[37] Rosenberg (1999, p. 118).

while profiting from establishing the Institutional Shareholder Service (ISS),[38] the first of its kind and the most prominent proxy-advisory firm to date. A close consideration of his arguments and career illuminates the evolution and consequences of institutional activism.

3.2.1 Compulsory Voting and Institutional Shareholders as Active Corporate Citizens?

Monks joined the DOL as Administrator of the Office of Pension and Welfare Benefit Programs in 1984. He was an aspiring politician and previously worked as a lawyer, businessman, and banker. According to Hilary Rosenberg, his biographer, "[t]he only reason Monks took this job was to advance his governance agenda," and "[h]is main concern [was] establishing the position that pension funds had fiduciary duties to act as owners of corporations."[39] From the beginning of his tenure, he intended to serve only one year as a pension administrator and to leverage his experience in government for a business career in corporate governance.[40]

In a speech "The Institutional Shareholder as a Corporate Citizen," later considered seminal among corporate governance activists, Monks told pension plan officers that

> it seems to me to be a self-evident proposition, that institutional shareholders have to be activist corporate citizens.... Given the huge blocks of stocks owned by institutions in all of our major companies, it is not always practical to quietly support management or ... sell if you don't approve of management's handling of the company. I would suggest that it behooves institutional shareholders, in the exercise of their corporate citizenship, to take the lead in proposing, and passing, provisions ... Even if you wanted to run away from a poorly managed company, you couldn't do it at once ... So like it or not, ... as a practical business matter, institutional shareholders are going to have to become more and more active shareholder-owners, and less and less passive investors[41]

Two aspects of this speech demand close attention: the call for stronger activism and the use of the term "owners." As to the first aspect, Monks took it for granted,

---

[38] Initially, its name was Institutional Shareholders Service. Monks changed the name to Institutional Shareholder Services in the same year (Rosenberg 1999, pp. 118–123).

[39] Rosenberg (1999, pp. 83–84).

[40] Rosenberg, borrowing Monks's own words, details this decision as follows: "On the taking the pension job, Monks vowed – to himself and his family – that he would stay in the position for just one year. ... he told his wife ... 'Trust me', he remembers saying to her ... 'I know my own temperament in the government. I have a single agenda for this. I'm not going into this because I want to be a career public servant. I'm going into this because it's in aid of my long-term project in trying to create change in the way that corporations function. I can't afford more than a year's time here'" (1999, p. 80).

[41] Rosenberg (1999, pp. 92–93).

as did later corporate governance activists, that with the growth of institutional shareholding, it had become more difficult for institutional shareholders to resort to the "Wall Street walk." The advocacy of stronger institutional activism was a corollary of this growing difficulty of selling their stakes.

From the perspective of the traditional regulations on institutional shareholders that encouraged diversification, however, this argument puts the cart before the horse. Diversification was encouraged to make it easier for institutional shareholders to take the Wall Street walk by selling off blocks of shares in a portfolio when the need would arise.[42] As institutional shareholding grew, the market for selling blocks of shares became more liquid, actually making it easier for an institutional shareholder to take the Wall Street walk by selling its shares to other institutional shareholders. Given the liquid stock market, there are no grounds to say that any particular institutional shareholder is "stuck" with certain portfolios. But Monks employed the growth of institutional shareholding *in aggregate* as a pretext for claiming that their shareholdings became illiquid and, therefore, stronger institutional activism was needed.

A crucial tactic in advancing this argument for stronger activism is to portray institutional shareholders as if they are homogeneous. They are, however, a diverse group that includes pension funds, mutual funds, university endowments, insurance companies, bank trusts, sovereign wealth funds, and other investment companies. Even among pension funds, over which Monks had influence as the chief US government pension administrator in 1984–1985, the investment objectives and approaches of private pension funds differed from one to another and from those of public pension funds. Institutional shareholders are, in general, competing fiercely with each other to improve trading performance and attract more customers. Treating them as a group and urging them to strengthen their activism regarding companies is tantamount to asking them to form an investor cartel. Moreover, as the growth of index funds demonstrates, institutional shareholders, in fact, evolved in the direction of being less interested in getting to know the affairs of individual companies closely. Diversification is still a main concern of most institutional shareholders. In their trading objectives and approaches, institutional shareholders have actually become more passive, contrary to their rhetorical activism, as will be discussed in Section 5.2.

As to the second point, it is an intentional misrepresentation for Monks to say that institutional shareholders are "owners" of corporations. However, they are fiduciaries or trustees of those households or organizations whose money they are managing. As a law student, Monks himself was clearly aware of this legal situation and used the term "fiduciaries" not infrequently in his writings and

---

[42] See Section 2.2.

speeches. But he liberally mixed "owners" and "fiduciaries" at his will and emphasized the former in his public statements.

For instance, in his remarks to *Institutional Investor* in 1984, Monks argued, "The only people who can change the contract under which corporations can function are the owners. And the owners are increasingly pension funds. . . . Is it part of a fiduciary responsibility to exercise the right to vote?"[43] This is in line with using the new term "shareholder-owners" in his speech, "The Institutional Shareholder as a Corporate Citizen" quoted above.

This rhetorical tactic to portray institutional shareholders as "owners" has successfully contributed later to the broad acceptance of a vertical relation of "owner versus manager," where corporate managers are agents of institutional shareholders who "own" the companies. As elaborated in Section 5.1, however, as soon as incorporation is done, nobody owns a corporation except the corporation, that is, the legal person itself. The corporation makes contracts with managers and issues securities to shareholders. Corporate managers are, therefore, business-managing fiduciaries who are entrusted by corporations, while institutional shareholders are money-managing fiduciaries who are entrusted by their clients. Thus, the relationship between corporate managers and institutional shareholders is horizontal between two fiduciaries serving different customers. Monks and other shareholder activists nonetheless distorted this relationship in public discourse and increasingly in the minds of policymakers, academics, and businesspeople.[44]

3.2.2 Institutional Shareholder Service (ISS) and the Proxy-Voting Business

Monk's other significant contribution to institutional activism and, later, to hedge-fund activism was establishing the proxy advisory firm ISS. He set up the company immediately after resigning from the DOL in 1985. He proposed the idea of ISS while he was the chief pension administrator, arguing in a December 1984 speech: "Current fiduciaries have neither the inclination nor the training to act as proprietors. Either they have to acquire them [capabilities to vote], or a new institution will be developed."[45] He later provided more details regarding this "new institution" at a DOL hearing, saying, "[i]t is time . . . for corporate, ERISA-covered pension fund sponsors and their managers to assign the vote to a third, neutral party."[46]

---

[43] Quoted in Rosenberg (1999, p. 92).

[44] In a similar vein, Blair (2003a) remarks: "The rhetoric of 'ownership', however subtly redefines corporations in terms of the presumed property rights of one class of participants in the firm, thereby adding a tone of moral superiority to the idea that corporates should be run in the sole interest of shareholders." (p. 57). See Section 5.4.

[45] Rosenberg (1999, p. 102).   [46] Rosenberg (1999, p. 103).

Monks was not simply an activist civil servant working for the public good. He was also a businessman who wanted to profit from his idea of "a third, neutral party." From the beginning, he already made it clear that he would stay with the DOL for only a year and then pursue his corporate-governance agenda in the business sector.[47] He later justified his personal profit-seeking as compatible with the public benefit with the analogy of a "double helix," one strand representing the "mission" and the other strand "money."[48] However, one fund manager directly admonished Monks for his conflicting interests in his campaign for a proxy-voting firm: "Monks, goddamn you. Guys like you, you go into government and start a forest fire and then you come and try to sell us all fire extinguishers."[49] According to his biographer Rosenberg, "Monks was astonished. Here was someone who saw right through him. He was indeed interested in selling the idea of a company that carried out voting tasks for funds."

Monks' "fire extinguishers" were beginning to be sold after he resigned from DOL in 1985. The regulatory authorities progressively defined voting as a fiduciary duty for institutional shareholders. The first of the changes, carried out by his colleagues remaining at the DOL, was the so-called "Avon letter" in 1988 that clarified the Department's position on the fiduciary duty of pension funds under ERISA.[50] This position was reiterated in "Statements on Pension Funds Investment" issued by the DOL and the Department of the Treasury in 1989.[51] Through these administrative directives, proxy voting was established as a fiduciary duty of pension fund managers. Thus, pension fund managers were required to vote in what they regarded as the "economic best interest of a plan's participants and beneficiaries."[52]

---

[47] Rosenberg (1999, p. 86).

[48] Pointing to the double helix structure of DNA, which consists of two strands of molecules arrayed as a twisted ladder, Monks said he wanted to "pursue the development of corporate governance through the structure of a profit-making business," explaining, "As a business, my idea had to be made relevant to people who were accustomed to paying only for something that was in fact valuable to them. I had to demonstrate that year in and year out good governance was good business. .... The parallel spiral forces of the double helix do not touch but are indispensable to each other" (Rosenberg 1999, p. 118).

[49] Rosenberg (1999, p. 117).

[50] The letter sent by a deputy assistant secretary at DOL to the Retirement Board of Avon Products Inc. stated as follows: "The decision as to how proxies should be voted with regard to the issues presented by the fact pattern are fiduciary acts of plan asset managers." In a subsequent speech, the then-assistant secretary of DOL asserted that "to meet this obligation, pension plan sponsors under ERISA must draw up detailed policies governing proxy voting and document all votes and the reasons behind them" (Rosenberg 1999, p. 165).

[51] The Avon letter has thus been "widely cited as the Labor Department's official position on fiduciary obligations of pension fund managers to vote the shares under their management" (Blair 2003a, p. 158).

[52] Blair (2003a, p. 158).

Before the issuance of these directives, the business of ISS had been stagnant because pension funds were not interested in paying money for ISS's service, although some might think it helpful.[53] With these new directives, however, pension funds faced the necessity of seeking professional advice from a "third, neutral party." The business of ISS then took off.[54]

The SEC extended the fiduciary duty of voting imposed on pension funds by DOL later to all other institutional shareholders, including mutual funds. In its ruling on proxy voting in 2003, the SEC made it clear that "an adviser is a fiduciary that owes each of its clients duties of care and loyalty . . ., including proxy voting" and that an adviser is required "to adopt and implement policies and procedures for voting proxies in the best interest of clients, to describe the procedures to clients, and to tell clients how they may obtain information about how the adviser has actually voted their proxies."[55] Until the SEC rule in 2003, ISS was virtually a monopoly proxy advisor. Sensing the growing market opportunity, Glass Lewis, currently the second-largest proxy advisory firm entered the proxy advisory market in the same year.[56]

Through his initiative to make institutional shareholders "active corporate citizens," Monks largely achieved his business ambition. After an investigation by the SEC for potential conflict of interest, he left ISS on paper in 1990, transferring $3 million worth of his shares in the company to an irrevocable trust and making his nephew and his son the trustees.[57] He then continued his corporate governance activism in the "double-helix" fashion by setting up corporate governance funds like the Lens Fund.[58] ISS successfully grew into a global company "operating worldwide across 25 global locations in 15 countries . . . [and serving] approximately 3,400 clients including many of the world's leading institutional investors." ISS maintains that "[with 3,000 employees, it] covers approximately 48,000 shareholder meetings in 115 markets, delivering proxy research and vote recommendations while working closely with clients to execute more than 12.8 million ballots representing 5.4 trillion shares."[59] The systemic effects of these changes will be discussed in Section 5.

---

[53] Blair (2003a, pp. 145–146).   [54] Blair (2003a, pp. 16–168).

[55] *See* Final Rule: Proxy Voting by Investment Advisers, 17 CFR Part 275, Release No. IA-2106 (February 11, 2003), www.sec.gov/rules/final/ia-2106.htm.

[56] It was originally set up by Canada's Ontario Teachers' Pension Plan and later acquired by Peloton Capital Management (PCM), a private equity, and Stephen Smith, the Chairman of PCM, in 2021. Refer to Glass Lewis press release on March 16, 2021, www.glasslewis.com/press-release-peloton-capital-management-and-stephen-smith-acquire-glass-lewis/ (Accessed on January 28, 2024).

[57] Rosenberg (1999, pp. 211–214).

[58] Corporate governance funds aim at increasing investment yields by applying pressure to improve corporate governance of their portfolio companies.

[59] ISS website (www.issgovernance.com/about/about-iss/, accessed on December 20, 2023).

3.3 Shareholder Activists Acting Together: The 1992 Proxy Rule Change and "Free Communication and Engagement"

While establishing proxy voting as a fiduciary duty of institutional share-holders, shareholder activists advocated for a proxy rule change that would make it easier for shareholders to aggregate their votes, allowing them to exert more influence on corporate management through freer communication between shareholders as well as freer engagement of shareholders with corporate management. Their concerted efforts resulted in the watershed SEC amendments to its proxy regulations in 1992.[60] Public pension funds, especially led the California Public Employees' Retirement System (CalPERS), and corporate raiders, through their umbrella organization, the United Shareholders Association (USA), collaborated closely to make the proxy rule change happen.

3.3.1 Public Pension Funds and Corporate Raiders

If Robert Monks was mainly an ideologue who promoted institutional activism through his corporate-governance agenda, public pension funds were its practitioners, taking direct action against corporations. This they did by bringing to bear their rights and influence as shareholders, setting up umbrella organizations for their activism, and lobbying the US government to change regulations in ways that would strengthen activism. They were "the most vocal advocates of corporate governance intervention" in the 1980s, and, conducting themselves as if they were rule-setters, they drafted codes of "best corporate governance practices" for their portfolio firms to adopt.[61]

From the 1950s, pension funds emerged as the biggest group of institutional shareholders in the United States because of the rapid expansion of business and government pension systems. By 1975, they held 16 percent of US corporate shares, four times more than mutual funds. Among them, private pension funds, although in aggregate a lot larger than public pension funds, were not interested in institutional activism. Most of them were run by business corporations on behalf of their employees, and it was unthinkable for their top managers to take activist positions against their own companies or other companies in general.[62]

---

[60] Calio and Zaharalddin (1994); Sharara and Hoke-Witherspoon (1993); Bainbridge (2005); 57 Fed. Reg. 48276, 48161–48304 (October 22, 1992).

[61] Cheffins (2013, p. 55).

[62] Corporate pensions held 13 percent of the market value of US corporate stocks whereas public pensions held 3 percent of the stocks in 1975. The corresponding figures were 20 percent and 5 percent, respectively, in 1985 and 18 percent and 8 percent in 1994. (Blair 1995, p. 46, Table 2.1)

Unlike corporate pensions, public pensions did not represent pensioners in the business sector and were hence freer to take an activist position regarding their portfolio companies. The retirement benefits of their clients, public-sector workers, were also more or less guaranteed by the state or federal government and they had relatively less sympathy with corporate-sector workers. This fact made them freer to favor shareholder interests over labor interests, when the two conflicted, even by advocating corporate restructuring led by corporate raiders that brought about layoffs and divestitures.[63]

Moreover, public pensions mostly held onto defined-benefit (DB) plans and were very slow to move to defined-contribution (DC) plans – a transition that occurred with increasing momentum at business corporations from the 1980s. DB plans expose the employer to the potential for underfunding of their pension plans, whereas DC plans do not. Public-pension fund administrators tried to avert this potential funding shortfall by using their collective shareholding power to seek higher yields from the stock market by strengthening shareholder activism. Public pension funds also had better access to regulatory authorities because they were regulated by states and exempted from the federal ERISA regime regulating private pension funds, and because a larger number of their administrators and board members were local administrators, politicians, labor unionists, and others. It was, therefore, relatively easy for them to effect regulatory changes that would allow them to increase the ratio of stock to other holdings in their investment portfolios and then use shareholder activism to seek higher yields on their portfolios.[64]

Among public pension funds, CalPERS emerged as the leader in institutional activism in the 1980s. As the largest pension fund in the US at the time, its significant holdings gave it the power to influence corporate boards.[65] Moreover, because it had become one of the most expensive pension systems,[66] CalPERS was pressured to boost its investment yields by expanding its investments in stock and actively influencing its portfolio companies.[67] Following California voters' approval of a 1966 ballot measure, CalPERS was allowed to invest up to 25 percent of its portfolio in stock. In 1984, that upper limit was removed completely.[68] This permissive regime contrasted with the restrictions placed on

---

[63] Gelter (2013, p. 40).   [64] See Gelter (2013).   [65] Smith (1996).

[66] Having introduced annual cost-of-living adjustments in 1968, two years later the fund adopted a very generous pension formula under which it paid 90 percent of their final salary for life to workers who retire at age 65 (Malanga 2013).

[67] In this context, Strine (2007) remarks, "Interestingly, some of the demand for outsized returns has come from institutional shareholders — such as public pension funds — facing actuarial risks because of underfunding and past investment mistakes" (p. 7).

[68] Malanga (2013). Early in the 1980s, CalPERS asked for permission to increase that limit to 60 percent. Although the voters rejected this proposal, they approved a different one in 1984 that allowed "CalPERS [to] expand its investments [in stock]," but refrained from specifying

other public pension funds, many of which had few or even no equities in their portfolios until the mid-1990s.[69]

Jesse Unruh, California's state treasurer from 1975 to 1987, was the principal catalyst in fashioning CalPERS into a leading institutional activist and establishing the Council of Institutional Investors (CII).[70] He was a politically powerful figure in his own right, noted by the *Wall Street Journal* as "the most politically powerful public finance officer outside the U.S. Treasury" due to his influence over Wall Street bankers.[71] Unruh consulted closely with Robert Monks to set up the CII as a platform for institutional shareholders to act together.[72] When CII was launched in 1985 as "the voice of corporate governance," its founders were 22 public and union pension funds, with California State Treasurer Jesse Unruh, New York City Comptroller Harrison J. Goldin, and State of Wisconsin Investment Board Chair John Konrad as founding co-chairs. CII later grew into a global organization comprising "more than 135 public, union and corporate employee benefit plans, endowments and foundations."[73]

In 1986, CalPERS started its major shareholder activist campaigns in close collaboration with CII. CalPERS led the campaigns by drafting a list of low-performing companies to help CII members to identify targets for their activist campaigns.[74] CalPERS also created a shareholders' bill of rights that included the one-share one-vote principle, demanded that corporations seek shareholder approval before paying greenmail or setting up poison pills, and called for a majority of outside directors to approve any extraordinary bonuses or other payments to corporate executives.

The most far-reaching shareholder action taken by CalPERS was the proxy rule amendment achieved in 1992. In 1989, CalPERS initiated the movement

---

a percentage limit and, for cosmetic purposes, put in "a clause that held CalPERS board members personally responsible if they didn't act prudently."

[69] Gelter (2013).   [70] Boyarsky (2007).

[71] Walters (1988). He earned this nickname because he had issued massive quantities of state-backed bonds through Wall Street bankers. Boyarsky (2007) describes him as having "transformed the job [of state treasurer which] used to garner as much political clout as the director of a local mosquito abatement district . . . into a source of financial and political power that reached from California to Wall Street" (p. 221). Uhlig (1987) also observed, "Because as Treasurer he was *ex officio* member of many California boards and commissions, Unruh oversaw 'the raising and expenditure of virtually all the state's money and consolidated his influence over billions of dollars in public investments and pension funds.'"

[72] Jesse Unruh closely cooperated with Monks about "the need for an assembly of large institutional shareholders" and helped him set up CII as a bipartisan organization. When Monks met with Unruh in 1984 to discuss the need for an assembly of large institutional shareholders, he said, "I thought it was a good idea, and I would give any Republican institutional support to the idea of forming an organization of institutional shareholders, but that . . . it should be bipartisan" (Rosenberg 1999, p. 100). On their encounter and cooperation, also refer to Boyarsky (2007, pp. 233–234).

[73] The CII website, www.cii.org/about (accessed on January 28, 2024).

[74] Smith (1996, pp. 231–223).

for the proxy-rule changes by sending a letter to the SEC that proposed forty-eight separate changes to the proxy rules, claiming that its main purpose was "to even the imbalance between shareholders and management concerning the filing and processing of proxy materials."[75]

The United Shareholder Association (USA), founded by corporate raider T. Boone Pickens in 1986 and purported to represent the interests of small shareholders, closely collaborated with public pension funds in making the proxy rule change happen.[76] The USA immediately followed up on the CalPERS letter about the proxy-rule change with its own letter to the SEC, arguing that "reform of the proxy process to allow shareholders a meaningful corporate governance role could forge a fundamental realignment of the now conflicting interests of management and shareholders . . . [S]uch realignment would maximize value on a constant basis, rather than through one-time restructuring transactions."[77]

After over three years' deliberation during which the SEC made two proposals and received comments from various groups and individuals in response, the SEC finalized the watershed amendments to its proxy regulations in 1992.[78] The USA declared "mission accomplished" and disbanded itself "shortly after the new SEC rules had been put in place."[79] Why were the amendments so important for shareholder activists, especially for corporate raiders?

3.3.2 The 1992 Proxy Rule Change and the Transformation of Corporate Raiders into Hedge-Fund Activists

The 1992 proxy rule change was a significant departure from the previous approach to proxy solicitation and communication among shareholders. Traditional regulations on public shareholders were unambiguous about prohibiting investor cartels and defined communication among investors as a proxy solicitation. It was, therefore, illegal for any shareholder to discuss company matters without first filing with and obtaining the approval of the SEC.[80]

---

[75] Sharara and Hoke-Witherspoon (1993, pp. 327, 336).

[76] The USA had already carried out various shareholder actions in parallel with those of CII. It produced an annual "Target 50" list of companies that were non-responsive to shareholders and attempted to negotiate with target companies to modify their governance structures to become more responsive to shareholder interests. It also mobilized its members' votes to sponsor proxy proposals if the target companies did not agree to its demands and augmented its shareholder activism in cooperation with CII. Several large institutional shareholders, such as CalPERS, the College Retirement Equities Fund (CREF), and the New York City Employees Retirement System (NYCERS), sponsored proposals on the USA's behalf. Refer to Strickland et al. (1996).

[77] Strickland et al. (1996, p. 337).

[78] SEC (1992); Sharara and Hoke-Witherspoon (1993); Bainbridge (2005).

[79] Blair (1995, p. 73). A quotation from Ralph V. Whitworth, "United Shareholders Association: Mission Accomplished," Remarks to Investor Responsibility Research Center Conference on Shareholder Management and Cooperation, October 27, 1993.

[80] Refer to Section 2.2.

The 1992 amendments, however, largely deregulated proxy communication, not only among shareholders but also with company management and the public.[81] This change subverted the spirit of the New Deal regulations in the name of allowing "market forces to restore a better sense of balance to America's board rooms" through the free flow of communication and engagement.[82]

The new rules loosened restrictions on public shareholders in three ways. First, shareholders were allowed to communicate freely with one another if each held less than 5 percent of its shares and had no special relationship with that company.[83] In other words, they were permitted to form shareholder cartels within the 5 percent limit. Second, with oral communications excluded from proxy regulation, shareholders were allowed to speak to or engage with management more freely.[84] This freer engagement resulted from accepting institutional shareholders' demand for more "active engagement" that would lead to "relationship investing."[85] Third, shareholders were given the freedom to make public statements on proxy-voting issues and to announce their voting intentions without violating the proxy-filing requirements.[86] With the 1992 rule amendment, the SEC distanced itself from the job of proxy censorship because it believed that contestants in proxy voting "should be free to reply to [an opponent's] statement in a timely and cost-effective manner, challenging the basis for the claims and countering with their views on the subject matter through the dissemination of additional soliciting material."[87]

In 1999, the SEC expanded the 1992 Rule 14a-12 and fully liberalized communication. Shareholders were now allowed to conduct unlimited solicitation among themselves and with the public, including through press releases, even if they abandoned proxy filing in the end.[88] This rule change allowed investors to engage more freely with corporate management

---

[81] Calio and Zaharalddin (1994, pp. 494–499); 17 C.F.R. § 240.14a-2(b) (2021).

[82] Calio and Zahralddin (1994, p. 466).   [83] 17 C.F.R. § 240.14a-2(b)(1) (2021).

[84] 1992 Final Rule, 17 C.F.R. § 240.14a-3.

[85] Sharara and Hoke-Witherspoon (1993, pp. 333–334). Blair (2003a) offers the definition of "relationship investing" as follows, "There is no agreement on a precise definition … but advocates most often describe it as a situation in which the investing institution is responsibly engaged in overseeing the management of the company, rather than remaining detached or passive … " (p. 172). Sharara & Hoke-Witherspoon (1993) also mention that "[r]elationship investing involves the creation of "an established, committed link between a company and one or more shareholders" and ranges from asking questions of board members to taking a seat on the board of directors and even assuming corporate debt" (p. 334).

[86] 17 C.F.R. § 240.14a-2(a)(1)-(2) (2021).   [87] 17 C.F.R. § 240.14a-2e(1) (2021).

[88] The new rules "do not require oral communications to be reduced to writing and filed … designed to reduce selective disclosure by permitting widespread dissemination of information through a variety of media calculated to inform all security holders about the terms, benefits and risks of a planned extraordinary transaction." Regulation of Takeovers and Security Holder Communications, Securities Act Release No. 7760, 64 Fed. Reg. 61,408 (November 10, 1999), www.sec.gov/rules/final/33-7760.htm.

and the public without being obligated to state their intentions in a legally binding document.[89] In particular, this rule allowed activist shareholders "to gauge the level of support from other shareholders" before filing a proxy statement and thereby "mitigate the risk of losing a costly proxy contest."[90]

The 1990s proxy-rule changes were crucial to transforming corporate raiders into hedge-fund activists. Corporate raiders were in retreat due to the collapse of the junk-bond market, with such prominent figures as Ivan Boesky and Michael Milken being jailed. State governments had passed regulations limiting hostile takeovers, and with devices such as the "poison pill," corporations had strengthened their defenses against corporate raiders. The sudden change in the market for corporate control in the late 1980s made corporate raiders scramble to find ways to maintain their business. In that situation, they thought the proxy rule change at the federal level was "one of the few remaining venues for effecting corporate management," and vigorously lobbied for it.[91]

More than anything else, the 1992 proxy rule amendment allowed corporate raiders to exert influence over corporate management by forming *de facto* shareholder cartels. When traditional proxy rules were in place, corporate raiders had to secure a significant shareholding in the company before they launched their campaign against corporate management, which was expensive and risky. With the introduction of anti-takeover measures in the late 1980s, the expense and risk of such campaigns increased further. However, the proxy-rule changes enabled them to influence management while holding only a tiny percentage of a corporation's stock. So long as they each held less than 5 percent, activists became free to communicate with each other and form a common front against their target company.

In contrast, management was left in the dark, not knowing the actual and potential size of the activists' coalitions. "Free engagement" has also strengthened the position of minority insurgents. After acquiring a small shareholding in the company, activists can freely engage with management and gauge its potential responses while expressing their concerns. "Free speech" has also bolstered activists: they are now free to criticize management through press conferences, websites, advertisements, and other means of public expression.[92]

As a result of the proxy-rule changes, activists' maneuvers became more "political." Previously, corporate raiders often employed takeover tactics, persuading other shareholders to sell them their shares, and then, armed with

---

[89] Briggs (2007).   [90] Lu (2016).   [91] Calio and Zahralddin (1994, pp. 460, 466).

[92] See the case of Third Point in Section 5.4 and that of Relational Investors and CalSTRS in Section 5.5.

a significant shareholding and a willingness to take over the target company eventually, they could determine its destiny. Hedge-fund activists, in contrast, needed to form a broad front by recruiting enough other shareholders to reach the level of voting power at which they could exert influence on the board. This process is equivalent to recruiting voters for political causes by establishing a common front to win an election. It should also be noted that there is a political advantage in acting against corporations as minority shareholders. Differentiating themselves from greedy corporate raiders willing to take over the whole company and strip its assets to increase their wealth, hedge-fund activists could portray themselves as weak "minority shareholders" victimized by management and promise justice for all shareholders. In this way, hedge-fund activists position themselves as proponents of shareholder democracy rather than those raiding corporations.[93]

3.4 Allowing Unlimited "Alternative Investment" in Hedge Funds: The 1996 NSMIA

Hedge funds, classified as *private funds*, are notable (and definable) primarily by their strategy of organizing *outside* existing financial regulations applicable to larger institutional funds. Because of this, hedge funds can employ trading strategies considered too speculative and therefore not allowed to institutional shareholders, and they conventionally utilize the "2 and 20" performance-pay scheme: an annual management fee of 2 percent of assets under management and a performance fee over the life of a particular fund of 20 percent of the profits in excess of a predetermined hurdle rate. Hedge funds and other private funds are structured specifically to avoid actions that would trigger certain disclosure rules and other regulations. For example, under the Securities Act of 1933, a fund seeking to be a private (i.e., unregistered) fund cannot publicly solicit prospective clients, the rationale being that "private placement" attracts informed, experienced investors.[94]

The gap between rhetoric and reality is most evident in hedge funds. The term "hedge fund" refers to managing a financial portfolio by "hedging" risks, a trading strategy originally adopted by Alfred Winslow Jones when he set up the first-ever hedge fund, A.W. Jones & Co., in 1949. However, the term has now been appropriated by speculators and manipulators who ply global financial markets in pursuit of "absolute returns" for themselves.[95]

---

[93] For more details on this transformation, see Lazonick and Shin (2020, pp. 133–155).

[94] Dayen (2016).

[95] Loomis (1966). The term "hedge fund" was coined by journalist Carol Loomis in 1966. As late as 2003 there was still no agreed definition of a hedge fund, though professional commentators would point to several characteristics of the funds: restricted access, performance fees, the ability to short, and the ability to leverage investments (Vaughn 2003). Section 404, of the 2010 Dodd-Frank Act created a provision to collect "systemic risk" data in the financial system of the United

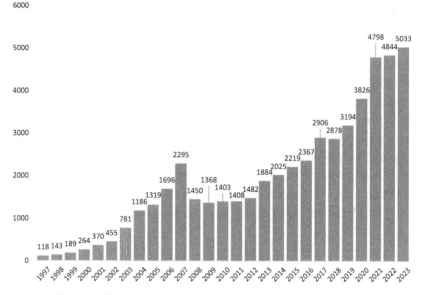

Figure 3 The growth of the hedge-hund industry, 1997–2023

Source: Statista (www-statista-com.libproxy1.nus.edu.sg/statistics/271771/assets-of-the-hedge-funds-worldwide, accessed on July31, 2023).

For nearly half a century after the launch of the first hedge fund, the hedge-fund industry grew anemically overall, experiencing periods of expansion and retraction.[96] From the 1990s, however, hedge funds exploded in size and number. The number of funds grew from around 610 in 1990 to about 11,000 in 2015. Their assets under management (AUM) grew from about $39 billion in 1990 to over $3 trillion in 2016 (Figure 3).[97]

States, modifying the Investment Advisors Act of 1940 such that the SEC, through form PF (private fund), has collected statistics on private funds (including hedge funds) in the United States since 2012. Hedge funds that must file form PF are described as private funds with one or more of the characteristics of charging "performance fees," using leverage to multiply investment scale, and engaging in short selling (Dodd-Frank Act 2011).

[96] A period of rapid growth had swelled hedge funds' ranks to an estimated number of 200 and their total assets to about $1.5 billion by the late 1960s; in subsequent years, however, fund failures or investor withdrawals ensued. See SEC (1969); Machan and Atlas (1994); Loomis (1970).

[97] Ahuja (2012); Dayen (2016). These estimates cannot necessarily be considered definitive, as in many cases they are based on voluntary disclosure by hedge funds and do not necessarily capture the entire universe of funds. The SEC suggests that in the second quarter of 2016 some 1,700 hedge-fund managers oversaw gross assets of $6.3 trillion (with net assets of $3.4 trillion) and 8,900 distinct funds (SEC 2017). Even here, not necessarily all hedge funds would be tracked, as the SEC is focused mainly on advisers of funds that have $150 million or more in AUM. In any case, the "average" fund manager might oversee as much as $3.7 billion. The 9,000 funds reported to the SEC would average as much as $654 million in gross AUM.

There were pull factors in this growth of the hedge-fund industry. In the early 1990s, some spectacular hedge-fund success stories became known to the public. One sensational story was the estimated $1 billion gain George Soros reaped on Black Wednesday in 1992 by "breaking the Bank of England" by shorting the British pound. Not only that. Soros Fund was reported to have generated an average annual return of more than 30 percent since its inception.[98] Hedge funds were beginning to be accepted as special investment vehicles that could create a persistent "alpha" – extra yield above the benchmark yield, although it is a matter of controversy whether they actually generate "alpha" for their clients.[99]

The explosive growth of the hedge-fund industry in the 1990s, however, had more to do with push factors that allowed the allocation of institutional share-holders' portfolios to hedge-fund investing as an "alternative investment" in their search for higher yields. The 1996 National Securities Markets Improvement Act (NSMIA), part of the Clinton administration's financial market deregulation, was crucial here. According to David Dayen, the regulatory change, "largely unnoticed at the time" and "advanced with broad Wall Street support and almost no resistance in Congress," effectively allowed hedge funds to draw unlimited financial resources from institutional shareholders without regulations that would have required disclosure of the firms' structure or prohibited overly speculative investments.[100]

Previously, to be exempt from regulation under the Investment Company Act of 1940, a hedge fund had to serve fewer than 100 "high-net-worth" investors, who were persons with a net worth of at least $1 million or who had generated an income of at least $200,000 annually for the previous two years. However, Section 209 of the NSMIA modified the Investment Company Act of 1940 to remove the long-existing regulation on the number of clients, creating an exemption for an unlimited number of "qualified purchasers," which could include any individual investor with a net worth of $5 million or more or any institutional shareholder with financial assets of $25 million or more.[101]

---

[98] Reiff (2017).

[99] For instance, the first comprehensive study of U.S. pension funds' investment in hedge funds, "All That Glitters Is Not Gold" conducted by the Roosevelt Institute, examined hedge-fund performance for eleven large public pensions in the United States over 88 fiscal years (eight fiscal years for each pension fund) and concluded that hedge-fund investment actually resulted in "high costs with low returns" (Parisian and Bhatti 2016). From 2001, CalPERS was in the vanguard among U.S. pension funds in allocating a portion of its portfolio to hedge-fund investment, but it announced in 2014 that it could no longer justify investing in hedge funds because of "its high costs and complexity." In earlier empirical research on hedge-fund performance, Stulz (2007) concluded that the persistent existence and size of alpha in hedge-fund investment was at best "controversial."

[100] Dayen (2016).

[101] 1940 Act, 15 U.S.C §§80a-2a (51)(A)(i)(iv). Existing regulations under the 1934 Securities Exchange Act would force registration with the SEC when and if the total number of investors

As such, NSMIA continued to treat hedge funds as private entities while granting them the ability to draw funds from a substantially larger pool of investors, most notably from institutional shareholders. As will be discussed in Section 5.5, the infusion of funds from institutional shareholders into hedge funds enabled their "co-investments" in target companies and inflated the power of activist hedge funds against them.

As Figure 3 shows, it took only seven years after the enactment of the NSMIA for hedge funds' assets under management (AUM) to increase more than tenfold, from $118 billion in 1997 to over $1.2 trillion in 2004. Since then, they more than doubled to over $3 trillion in 2016 and again nearly doubled to $5.1 trillion in 2022. The main contributor to this explosive growth of hedge funds' AUM was the alternative investment by institutional shareholders following the 1996 NSMIA. According to Preqin Global Hedge Fund Report, about 60 percent of hedge-fund assets in 2015 came from more than 5,000 institutional shareholders. Leading institutional funds were public and private pension funds and endowments, representing about 53 percent of hedge funds' total assets.[102]

The rise of hedge-fund activism was a phenomenon that reflected the explosive growth of the overall hedge-fund industry. The combined AUM of activist hedge funds increased more than tenfold in six years, from $15 billion in 1997 to $117 billion in 2003, and then more than quadrupled in the next 11 years, to reach $507 billion in 2014, as Figure 4 shows.[103]

Both the incidence of activist campaigns and their success ratio increased sharply. Schedule 13D filings with the SEC are often used as a proxy for activist campaigns because a 13D must be filed when an investor accumulates a 5 percent-or-greater share of a corporation's outstanding stock, which also triggers a requirement that the investor discloses the purpose of its accumulation.[104] The incidence of 13D filings for activist purposes increased

---

reached 500 or if total assets exceeded $10 billion. In practice, then, the post-NSMIA environment created a "threshold" for hedge funds and an incentive to limit their population of investors to no more than 499 institutions or very wealthy individuals.

[102] Preqin (2016).

[103] Lazonick and Shin (2020, p. 131). Following the SEC's (2017) convention of including "distressed/restructuring" assets and "risk arbitrage/merger arbitrage" assets in "event-driven" assets, Lazonick and Shin estimated the AUM of activist hedge funds by combining "event-driven" assets, "distressed" assets] and "merger arbitrage" assets in BarclayHedge data above. The numbers then become similar to those of the SEC where the overall size of "event-driven" assets is $430 billion. Foley (2016), Foley and Johnson (2014), Marriage (2013), and Chandler (2016) also equate activist assets with the overall assets devoted to an event-driven strategy. The overall trend in the growth of hedge fund activists' AUM is more or less the same in those estimates.

[104] For instance, an investor should disclose whether it demands a change in management, stock buybacks or special dividends, a seat on the board, and so on. In contrast, investors file schedule 13G when assuming a *passive* stake of 5 percent or more in a publicly traded corporation.

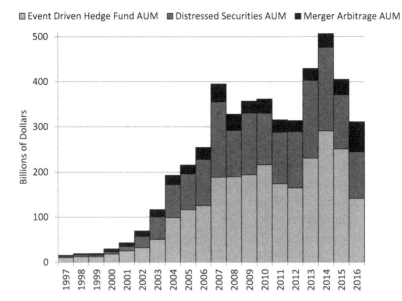

Figure 4 The expansion of hedge-fund activists, by type of fund, 1997–2016
Source: Lazonick & Shin (2020, p. 131, Figure 6.2).

from 10 in 1994 to 212 in 1997.[105] It then increased to 353 in 2008. After a sharp reduction during the Global Financial Crisis of 2008–2009, the incidence recovered to 355 in 2015. In 2003, 39 percent of proxy fights for board seats resulted in settlements or victories for activists; this success rate soared to 60 percent in 2013.[106] The growth of hedge funds, the growth of activist hedge funds, and the increasing success rate of hedge-funds' activist intervention were phenomena that happened in parallel since the introduction of the 1996 NSMIA.

3.5 Agency Theory and the Maximizing Shareholder Value View (AT-MSV)

Social movements progress with ideologies to legitimize them. For shareholder activism, the legitimization was provided by agency theory and its maximizing shareholder value view (AT-MSV henceforth),[107] which emerged as a new

---

[105] The SEC requires purchasers of corporate stock to file form 13D within 10 days of the date on which their ownership stake crosses the 5 percent threshold. The form requires disclosure of the intent of the acquisition of stock.

[106] Lazonick and Shin (2020, p. 131, Figure 6.3).

[107] Scholars often mix agency theory and the MSV view without clarifying the relationship between the two. When they are applied to the relationship between shareholders and managers, the MSV view is a corollary of agency theory, stating that "managers should maximize

branch of neoclassical economics in the middle of the 1970s when corporate raiders were beginning to make their marks. The AT-MSV argument runs in the following manner: (1) Corporate managers are agents of shareholders who are (ultimate) owners of the corporation, and they are responsible for maximizing the value of their principals, that is, shareholders; (2) If managers act entirely as agents of shareholders by focusing solely on maximizing shareholder value, corporate performance as well as the efficiency of the economy would improve. (3) Managers, however, try to maximize their own benefits as self-interested agents and tend to build their own fiefdoms (at the expense of their principals), resulting in agency costs. One way to reduce this "agency cost" is to increase stock-related compensation for corporate executives because it will align their incentives to shareholders.[108]

Although it had logical and empirical fragilities, as discussed in Section 5.1, AT-MSV provided shareholder activism with strong academic support. First, AT-MSV's principal-agent relationship between public shareholders and corporate managers established the primacy of the latter and bolstered the confidence of shareholder activists. It elevated public shareholders to the status as if they could make an order to managers, "You should strive to maximize my value wholeheartedly. That is your mission!" Combined with Robert Monks' push for portraying institutional shareholders as "owners" of corporations,[109] AT-MSV helped the relationship between institutional shareholders and corporate managers increasingly be accepted as a vertical one where the latter is an agent of the formers. However, their legal relationship is horizontal in that institutional shareholders are "money-managing fiduciaries" serving their clients, whereas corporate managers are "business-managing fiduciaries" serving their corporations, as will be discussed in Section 5.1.

AT-MSV justified this principal-agent relationship with the "residual claimant" argument in that it is only shareholders who make risky investments in the corporation's productive assets without guaranteed returns, and therefore, it is only shareholders who have a claim on the corporation's profits, if and when they occur.[110] Although this argument is fraught with logical and empirical

---

shareholder value because they are agents of shareholders." I therefore use an abbreviation, AT-MSV, for "agency theory and the MSV view."

[108] See generally Jensen and Meckling (1976); Fama (1980); Fama and Jensen (1983); Jensen (1986, 1988, 1993); Jensen and Murphy (1990).

[109] Refer to Section 3.2.

[110] For instance, Fama and Jensen (1983) state: " . . . the least restricted residual claims in common use are the common stocks of large corporation. Stockholders are not required to have any other role in the organization [and therefore not paid by any other contracts with the organization]; their residual claims are alienable without restriction; and because of these provisions, the residual claims allow unrestricted risk sharing among stockholders" (p. 303). Also refer to Lazonick (2019, pp. 53–68); Lazonick and Shin (2020, pp. 187–89).

weaknesses, it offered justification for corporate raiders' and later hedge-fund activists' push for increasing dividend payouts and stock buybacks as their rightful claims.[111]

Combined' with establishing the primacy of public shareholders through the principal-agent relationship, AT-MSV's depiction of the relationship as a conflicting rather than a cooperating one offered strong support for shareholder activism to place managers under the control of shareholders. Jensen (1986) emphasizes: "Payouts to shareholders reduce the resources under managers' control, thereby reducing managers' power ... Managers have incentives to cause their firms to grow beyond the optimal size. Growth increases managers' power by increasing the resources under their control" (p. 323). Fama's (1980) model is also based on the manager's tendency of "shirking" or appropriating "perquisites": " ... a manager has an incentive to consume more on the job than is agreed in his contract. The manager perceives that ... he can beat the game by shirking or consuming more perquisites than previously agreed" (p. 296).

AT-MSV, therefore, explained hostile takeovers led by corporate raiders, or what was more generally known as "the market for corporate control," as one way to improve corporate performance by forcing managers to stop wasting corporate resources and by "disgorging" the corporation's "free cash flow" to shareholders. Jensen (1988) argues, "Increase in financial flexibility that gives managers control over free cash flow may actually cause the value of the firm to decline" and takeover activities accompanied with the increase in debts, that is, leveraged buyouts would "motivate managers to disgorge the cash rather than invest it at below the cost of capital or waste it through organizational ineffi-ciencies" (p. 29).

At the same time, AT-MSV legitimized making stock-based pay an important proportion of executive compensation because it would supposedly align the incentives of corporate managers in allocating resources with those of public shareholders.[112] Based on their assumption of the entirely egoistic CEO that "[he] compares only his private gain and cost from pursuing a particular activ-ity," Jensen and Murphy (1990) argue, "compensation policy that ties the CEO's welfare to shareholder wealth helps align the private and social costs and benefits of alternative actions and thus provides incentives for CEOs to take appropriate actions" (p. 226).

Following AT-MSV's advice and the insistence of shareholder activists, companies substantially increased executives' stock-based pay. According to Frydman and Jenter (2010), the S&P 500 CEO's average pay increased from $1.2 million in the 1970s to $1.8 million in the 1980s, $4.1 million in the 1990s,

---

[111] Details will be discussed in Section 5.1.   [112] Jensen and Murphy (1990).

and $9.2 million in 2000–2005 in 2000 constant dollars.[113] A significant part of this steep pay increase was due to the increase in stock-based pay. The portion of stock-based pay to CEOs' total compensation was 13 percent in the 1960s and 16 percent in the 1970s. It then increased sharply to 26 percent in the 1980s, 37 percent in the 1990s, and 60 percent in 2000–2005. This increase in stock-based pay opened a room to make executives susceptible to the pressure from hedge-fund activists to increase stock buybacks, as will be discussed in Sections 4.2 and 5.1.

4 Evaluation of Institutional Activism and Hedge-Fund Activism

More than three decades have passed since institutional activism began in the United States, and there has been voluminous literature on assessing its impacts on corporate performance and share prices. Section 4.1 examines the two recent comprehensive survey articles on empirical research, Denes et al. (2017) and deHaan et al. (2019), and critically analyzes Bebchuk et al. (2015), Brav et al. (2010) and Brav et al. (2015) that are supportive of hedge-fund activism. It points out that, among empirical researchers in this field, it is already well-established that institutional activism did not contribute to improving corporate performance and stock prices in the long run. It then argues that it is inconclusive whether hedge-fund activism has long-run positive impacts on corporate performance and share prices if we carefully re-examine the existing empirical research. Section 4.2 examines the flow of funds between the stock market and the corporate sector and argues that "predatory value extraction," value extraction far in excess of contribution to value creation, was more likely to happen with the rise of shareholder activism.

4.1 The Recent Empirical Research on Institutional Activism and Hedge-Fund Activism

In 'Thirty years of Shareholder Activism: Survey of Empirical Research,' Denes et al. (2017) summarize the results of the empirical research as follows: (1) shareholder activism was in general effective in bringing about some organizational changes in target firms; (2) shareholder proposals and negotiations by institutional shareholders are ineffective in changing target firms' stock prices and earnings; (3) but shareholder activism by hedge-funds was effective in changing target firms' stock prices and earning in the short run, especially when it is combined with hedge funds' purchase of relatively large block of shares; (4) following hedge-fund activism, target firms tended

---

[113] The numbers here are only rough estimates. According to Hopkins and Lazonick (2016), there are only reasonably consistent data on the correct realized gains on CEO pay from 1992 in the U.S.

"to decrease their capital expenditures, increase their payouts, and increase their incidence of asset divestitures, restructurings, or employee layoffs,"[114] (5) studies that claim long-term effects of shareholder activism is mixed: The effects on stock returns are "statistically insignificant" while "hedge fund activism is associated with increases in operating performance."[115]

Findings (1) and (2) had been well established by the early 2010s. One of the authors of the paper above, Karpoff (2001), already reported a survey result that institutional activism had "negligible effects on target companies" in terms of "share values, earnings, or operations" while it prompted "small changes in target firms' governance structures" (p. 1). Gillan and Starks (2007) provided similar survey results on institutional activism. Brav et al. (2010), who are supportive of hedge-fund activism, also made it clear that they concurred with Gillan and Starks (2007) and said that was why they focused their empirical research on hedge-fund activism.

Findings (3) and (4) are also hardly disputed. Compared with activist institutional shareholders frequently exposed to a conflict of interests,[116] hedge-fund activists make single-minded interventions to increase their financial gains through stock-price manipulation, cost reductions, and other restructuring measures. Moreover, hedge-fund activists have substantially strengthened their power, and it has become increasingly difficult for corporate management to ignore their demands, as discussed in Sections 3.3 and 3.4. Therefore, finding (5) – the long-term effects of hedge-fund activism on share prices and operating profits – is the only remaining issue to be resolved.[117]

In 'Long-Term Economic Consequences of Hedge Fund Activist Interventions,' deHaan et al. (2019) delve into the issue (5). Their conclusions are identical to those of Denes et al. (2017) in rejecting the claim of positive effects on long-term stock returns. So, the change in long-term operational profits is the only controversial issue that needs to be resolved. They closely examine 11 papers that Denes et al. (2017) surveyed on operational performance, including Bebchuk et al. (2015), Brav et al. (2010), and Brav et al. (2015).[118] They then reject the hypothesis that hedge-fund activism brought about long-term positive effects on operational performance.

---

[114] Denes et al. (2017, p. 411).   [115] Denes et al. (2017, pp. 410, 411).

[116] Refer to discussions in Section 5.4.

[117] There are many other studies that are not supportive of hedge-fund activism including Briggs (2007), Cheffins and Armour (2011), Coffee and Palia (2016), and Becht et al. (2017). Here I focus on critically examining those supportive of hedge-fund activism.

[118] To be sure, Bebchuk et al. (2015) emphasize that they target the 'myopic-activists claim' that "activist interventions are followed by short-term gains that come at the expense of subsequent long-term declines in operating performance" and they "find no evidence to support the concerns" (p. 1117). The paper is however often cited as empirical research to show the positive long-term effects on operating performance because people tend to stress the latter half of the

First, deHaan et al. (2019) point out that the previous studies claiming the positive effects only examined the post-activism performance without comparing it with the pre-activism performance. Considering the pre-activism trend is critical because the improvement in operational efficiency during the period after the activist intervention may simply reflect the trend of operational improvement already set before the intervention. deHaan et al. (2019, pp. 541, 554) took the pre-activism performance into account and compared the performance of the initial year with the post-activism performance. They then find no evidence of abnormal post-activism performance improvement and reject the hypothesis.

Second, deHaan et al. (2019) also raise questions about employing returns on assets (ROA) as a measurement of operational efficiency after activist interventions. All eleven studies cited in Denes et al. (2017) focus on ROA, and some of them supplement their findings with other measures such as Tobin Q, FSCORE, and ROE (returns of equities). deHaan et al. (2019) mildly criticize this convention of the previous researchers by remarking, "ROA only provides a partial view of a firm's operating efficiency. For example, a target's ROA may be inflated because the denominator has shrunk due to cash payouts, even though its use of operating assets has not changed" (p. 544).

In my view, this is a more serious matter. I suspect that the predominance of relying on ROA may have to do with the relative ease of "proving" the supposed positive effects of hedge-fund activism. Take a look at Denes et al.'s (2017) summary of the previous studies on operational changes after activist interventions in finding (4) above: "Following such activism, target firms tended to decrease their capital expenditures, increase their payouts, and increase their incidence of asset divestitures, restructurings, or employee layoffs" (p. 413). It is then more likely that the increase in ROA was due to the decrease in the denominator (asset) through asset divestitures, decrease in capital expenditure, restructuring, and layoffs without the increase in the numerator (net profit). It is misleading to interpret the ROA increase itself as an operational improvement of a company.

Third, there is an even more severe problem of the empirical studies purporting long-term operational efficiency improvement, which deHaan et al. (2019) do not point out. It has to do with flaws in their dataset. For instance, Bebchuk et al. (2015, pp.1099, 1090) claim to provide "the first systematic evidence on the long-term effects of hedge fund activism" by using a dataset consisting of

---

result in the quotation as follows: "Following the month of partial cashing out by the activists, there is no evidence for negative abnormal returns in the subsequent three years. Indeed, returns in this period are positive, though not always statistically significant, in many specifications" (p. 1134).

"the full universe of approximately 2,000 interventions" and by examining the effects during the five years after the interventions. However, almost half of the firms disappeared from the Compustat database that they used to calculate changes in earnings. In the case of ROA, the number of firms that remained in Compustat declined from 1,584 in the year of the 13D filing to 815 five years later, and in the case of Tobin's Q (the measure of the firm's market value to book value), the decline was from 1,611 to 831.[119]

Bebchuk et al. (2015, p. 1104) assert that "most of the disappearances from Compustat [were] due to acquisitions." But they do not provide any evidence to support it. They only claim, "When we compare the target firms to peer companies matched by size and performance, we find that the matched firms also have a high attrition rate of 42% within five years; most disappearances from Compustat are again due to acquisitions." As they do not tell us whether they documented acquisitions among the "peer companies," which is unlikely, their claim is just their surmise. They only mention "the acquirer's expectation" of the improvement to support their surmise in a footnote.[120] Without documenting why nearly half of the firms in the dataset disappeared, asserting that they did so primarily by acquisitions is not a tenable academic proposition.

A company disappears from a dataset of listed companies for various reasons: It may go out of business, fail to maintain the minimum listing requirements of the stock market, or be acquired by another company. It will be more reasonable to suppose the average performance of surviving companies in the stock market after five years is generally better than that of all the companies listed in the first year. The initial average performance of bankrupt companies, or those failing to maintain the minimum listing requirement, is likely lower than that of surviving companies. This survival effect will be more substantial if the number of disappearing companies is high, such as Bebchuk et al.'s dataset, where nearly half of companies disappeared after five years. It is not reasonable to use the higher average performance of the surviving companies as evidence that the overall performance of the initial group has improved.

---

[119] Lazonick and Shin (2020, Chapter 7).

[120] Bebchuk (2015, p. 1085, footnote 124) again surmises as follows: "Indeed, acquisitions can often be expected to be motivated by the acquirer's expectation that it will be able to improve the performance of the purchased assets through synergies or otherwise. To the extent that this is the case, it can be expected that the performance of assets of activism targets that are acquired will tend to improve, rather than decline, after the targets are acquired and stop having their operating performance reported on Compustat." There are however numerous failure cases of M&As. Moreover, even if operational efficiency were improved after the acquisition, it was due more likely to the effect of acquisition than that of hedge-fund activism. Whether the acquisition was due to hedge fund interventions or not and whether hedge fund interventions improved operational efficiency via acquisition are matters to verify separately.

A re-examination of the empirical research discussed above does not support long-term performance improvement from shareholder activism, both institutional and hedge-fund activism. The result is not surprising if one looks at the contents of hedge funds' demands on corporations. Their typical demands are to increase payouts to shareholders through stock buybacks and dividends, often accompanied by selling off assets and slashing costs. It is difficult to find a plausible reason why a company will achieve a long-run operational improvement and the consequent long-run stock price increase if its managers follow those demands. The only "theoretical" support for those demands comes from AT-MSV, as discussed in Section 3.5.

4.2 The Buyback Economy and Predatory Value Extraction

If we examine the flow of funds between corporations and shareholders, it will be more plausible to say that shareholder activism has resulted in "predatory value extraction" rather than simply not bringing about a long-run performance improvement. Two facts stand out from Figures 5 and 6, which show the flow of funds for 219 companies in the S&P 500 Index publicly listed from 1981 through 2019.

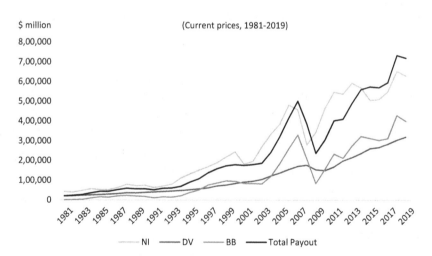

Figure 5 The trend of corporate income, stock buybacks, dividends, and total payout of S&P 500 companies (Value, US dollar)

Source: Standard and Poor's Compustat database; calculations by Mustafa Erdem Sakinç and Emre Gomeç of the Academic-Industry-Research Network in July 2023.

Note: Data are for 216 companies in the S&P 500 Index in February 2020 that were publicly listed from 1981 through 2019. BB: Buyback; NI: Net income; DV: Dividend payout; (BB+DV): Total payout.

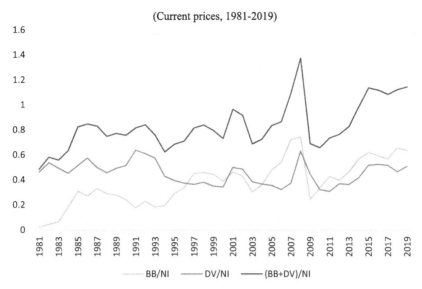

Figure 6 The trend of corporate income, stock buybacks, dividends, and total payout of S&P 500 companies (payout ratios)

Source & Notes: Same as those in Figure 5.

First, the total payout to shareholders (inclusive of dividends and stock buyback) has continued to increase, and currently, almost all the net income of S&P companies is paid to shareholders. It comprised 48.5 percent of their net income in 1981, and the total payout ratio rose to 114.4 percent in 2019. The rapid and steady growth of the payout ratio can be viewed better by examining the trend of the average payout ratio over decades. The ratio in the 1980s (1981–1989) was 69.7 percent. It then rose to 76.1 percent in the 1990s (1990–1999), 88.8 percent in the 2000s (2000–2009), and 95.7 percent in the 2010s (2010–2019). Many S&P companies "routinely distribute more than 100% of their net income to shareholders."[121]

Second, the increase in stock buybacks accounts for nearly all the payout ratio rise. At the beginning of the 1980s, buybacks were minimal, comprising only 2.2 percent of the net income of the S&P 500 companies, and the buyback portion of net income increased to 63.5 percent in 2019. Over the past three decades, the dividend increase was nearly proportional to the corporate profit increase. The dividend ratio was 49.9 percent on average in the 1980s, 47.5 percent in the 1990s, 42.1 percent in the 2000s, and 43.1 percent in the 2010s. But the buyback ratio, recording 19.9 percent on average in the 1980s, rose to 28.5 percent in the 1990s, 46.7 percent in the 2000s, and 52.5 percent in the 2010s.

---

[121] Lazonick (2019, p. 48).

We should pay particular attention to the sharp increase in stock buybacks to understand the extent and contents of predatory value extraction. Traditionally, companies used to justify stock buybacks for other reasons, for instance, to keep them as reserves to reward their employees and executives, use them as currencies for stock-swap M&As, and defend stock prices when market conditions are unfavorable. With the strengthening of shareholder activism, however, companies have increasingly justified buybacks as a "shareholder-friendly measure," "returning excess cash to shareholders," or even "returning capital to shareholders." Hedge-fund activists' demand for stock buybacks is also justified as a shareholder-friendly measure. Section 4.1. pointed out that there is no plausible economic theory that the contents of shareholder activists' demands would improve the operational efficiency of companies in the medium and long run. The same can be said about stock buybacks, which is the main content of the activists' demands.

Stock buybacks are simply a shift of corporate assets from one form to another because a company purchases its shares in the open market by paying its reserves. There is no intrinsic value difference between when it keeps money as reserves and converts the equivalent amount into its shares through buybacks. Stock buybacks can increase the corporate value only when they correctly time the repurchasing of shares at prices below their intrinsic value and keep them until the stock prices are recovered. However, major US companies tended to do buybacks in bull markets, for example, when share prices were high rather than low. Their buybacks, therefore, should not be understood as investments in their own undervalued shares.[122] Why do we then see the buyback spree?

It has to do with the fact that stock buybacks change two things: short-term demand for its shares and its earnings per share (EPS). First, they create extra demand for a company's shares in the stock market. This effect is more substantial when the scale of buybacks is bigger. Second, buybacks increase a company's earnings per share (EPS) without increasing overall earnings because they decrease the number of outstanding shares, the denominator of the EPS calculation. Market participants often accept the increase in EPS as an improvement in corporate efficiency without carefully examining whether the change has come from the numerator or the denominator.

After the announcement of stock buybacks by a company, the combination of the short-term demand increase for shares and the EPS increase tends to result in a short-term increase in share prices.[123] The empirical research on the effect of

---

[122] Lazonick (2014b).

[123] Lazonick and Jacobson (2022) identifies a four-stage buyback process through which open market repurchases can boost a company's stock price at the following junctures: (1) when the company announces a program to do share repurchases; (2) when the firm's broker actually

stock buybacks mostly confirms short-term share price increases after the announcement of stock buybacks, although the effect is not conclusive on the long-term share price increase.[124] This result is consistent with the empirical research on shareholder activism discussed in Section 4.1, as one of the most frequent requests by hedge-fund activists is stock buybacks.[125]

Lazonick (2014b) points out that this short-term movement of stock prices principally benefits share*sellers*, not share*holders*. Those who sell shares can safely realize capital gains when the share price increases as the company continues to repurchase them from the stock market for a given period. Those who hold shares beyond the repurchase period do not benefit from stock buybacks because the company's intrinsic value does not change. It should be noted that those who can benefit from the window of selling opportunity are limited to those with access to information and the capability to time the trading. They include hedge-fund activists who instigated stock buybacks after buying shares with an expectation that companies would acquiesce to their demands and senior executives who are involved in making decisions on stock buybacks and can benefit from the timing of stock option exercises and the vesting of stock awards.

Corporate executives became susceptible to stock buybacks from the 1980s for two major reasons. First, the introduction of Rule 10b-18 of the Securities Exchange Act in 1982, a "safe harbor" clause, allowed management to buy a significant number of the company's shares in the open market on any given business day without fear that the SEC would charge them with stock-price manipulation.[126] Second, ever since the broad adoption of stock-based pay for

---

executes the buybacks on the open market, which may be done trading day after trading day; (3) when the upward momentum that buybacks give to a company's stock price is reinforced by market speculation that the stock-price increase will continue; and (4) when the company releases its quarterly earnings report, with buybacks resulting in a higher EPS, even if earnings have failed to increase. These four stages in the buyback process can reinforce one another in lifting a company's stock price.

[124] See Manconi et al. (2018) and Ayres and Olenick (2017).

[125] I suspect that empirical studies that appear to support the long-term stock price increase may have technical and methodological problems to support their claims, as those that support the long-term positive effect of hedge-fund activism. For instance, Manconi et al. (2019) point out that " ... long-term excess returns are an anomaly, and anomalies can be the result of data mining or chance. Moreover, recent studies argue that the long-term returns can be explained by takeover activity or may compensate investors for takeover risk exposure and thus do not create value" (p. 1900).

[126] Management is not liable to the charge of stock-market manipulation provided, among other things, that the amount does not exceed a "safe harbor" of 25 percent of the previous four weeks' average daily trading volume. The SEC requires companies to report total quarterly repurchases but not daily ones, meaning that it cannot determine whether a company has breached the 25 percent limit without a special investigation. Even within the 25 percent limit, companies can still make huge purchases. For instance, Exxon Mobil could buy back about $300 million worth of shares a day, and Apple up to $1.5 billion a day. Therefore,

corporate executives starting in the 1980s, they have been paid heavily through stock options and stock awards, which ranged between 60 percent and 86 percent of the total remuneration for the 500 highest-paid executives between 2006 and 2015.[127] EPS also became an important metric to determine their salaries because stock options and stock awards can be exercised when EPS hits certain targets.[128]

Before the 1980s, the growth rate of real wages tracked that of labor productivity. From the 1980s, however, the gap between the two has continued to increase, with the former falling further behind the latter.[129] The corporate reserves spent on buybacks could have been used to provide increased job stability and higher earnings to the broad base of employees who helped generate the company's profits. Instead, by raising the gains of those privileged share*sellers*, buybacks contributed to the widening income gap.[130] This process of concentration of income in the hands of a small number of people has undergone over the last three decades and contributed to the decline of the American middle class and the emergence of the "1 percent versus 99 percent" framework in income distribution.

5 Why Has Shareholder Activism Gone Astray?

In 2013, toward the end of his long career as a corporate-governance activist, Monks admitted in an interview, "It's broke," adding: "Ownership is a fiction, governance a mirage."[131] In a speech prepared in 2015, he also acknowledged, "The fundamental dynamics of Corporate Governance have been diluted into virtual meaninglessness."[132] He observed the situation correctly that institutional activism had gone astray because it became evident in the early 2010s that institutional activism failed to achieve its stated objectives, as discussed in Section 4.1.

Monks, however, attributed the failure mainly to the power of "manager-kings" and the passivity of institutional shareholders: "These trustees likely hold more than 50% of the voting shares of each of the Fortune 500, yet their influence is negligible *by choice*. So we have a controlling percentage of public companies in the hands of trustees who act powerlessly in the arena of the

---

Lazonick argues that "[I]n essence, Rule 10b-18 legalized stock market manipulation through open-market repurchases" (Lazonick 2014b, pp. 46–55). Also refer to 17 CFR § 240.10b-18 (2021).

[127] Hopkins and Lazonick (2016).

[128] In a survey of corporate executives, for instance, Brav et al. (2005) find that 75 percent of CFOs claim that increasing EPS is an "important" or "very important" factor in stock buyback decisions (p, 483; 501–503). Cheng et al. (2015) also find that "when a CEO's bonus is directly tied to EPS, his company is more likely to conduct a repurchase and the magnitude of the repurchase tends to be larger" (pp. 447– 448).

[129] Lazonick and Shin (2020, p. 2, Figure 1.1).

[130] Lazonick and Shin (2020, pp. 3–4, Figure 1.2).   [131] Monks (2013).   [132] Monks (2015).

manager-kings."[133] This kind of diagnosis, a mantra of shareholder activists still widely present in corporate governance discourses, only calls for shareholders' stronger activism and making recalcitrant management susceptible to their demands. However, the recipe did not work so far, as discussed in Section 4. After the failure of institutional activism became evident in the early 2010s, hedge-fund activism has become stronger. Unlike institutional activism, which is exposed to conflicts of interest, hedge-fund activism is devoted to the single-minded pursuit of financial gains for shareholders. Nonetheless, it has also gone awry.

We should examine more carefully why shareholder activism arrived at the current state. It is of no use to blame individual actors, whether they are powerful CEOs or passive institutional shareholders, for the failure. We should investigate systemic reasons if we want to draw constructive solutions. In this section, we deal with those reasons in detail. First, the most fundamental is the lack of a theory about the actual relationship between institutional shareholders and corporations. Shareholder activism has been theoretically supported only by AT-MSV, which does not have convincing explanations of how companies operate and create value (Section 5.1). Second, contrary to shareholder activists' expectations, institutional shareholders, in general, evolved into entities that are uninterested in and incapable of corporate voting, although their voting power has become stronger and more concentrated. Characteristics of institutional shareholding strayed from the ideal of shareholder democracy (Section 5.2). Third, by imposing voting a fiduciary duty of these uninterested and incapable institutional shareholders, a large vacuum was created in the arena of corporate voting that hedge-fund activists could easily exploit for their profits while increasing the illegitimate influence of proxy advisory firms such as ISS (Section 5.3). Fourth, the proxy rule changes in the 1990s aiming at "free communication and engagement" made it easier for hedge-fund activists to aggregate dispersed votes and take actions for predatory value extraction (Section 5.4). Fifth, the predatory value extraction became exacerbated because hedge-fund activists could gain more power by "co-investments" with institutional shareholders (Section 5.5).

5.1 Confusion between Value Creation and Value Extraction

The problems that corporations are perceived to have are associated with one of two phenomena: value creation and value extraction. Value creation is a process of creating corporate value by improving operational performance.

---

[133] Monks (2013). My emphasis. He even contends that "Capitalism has become a kleptocracy, run by and for the enrichment of CEOs, or what I term 'manager-kings.' So powerful have these manager-kings become, they now bend the will of governments, effectively capturing the power of state democratic institutions."

It is mainly a domain of corporate management: Managers try to achieve better operational performance by generating high-quality, low-cost goods and services, for which they combine strategic control, organizational integration, and financial commitment. This capability to innovate by overcoming uncertainties is called managerial capability.[134]

On the other hand, value extraction is a process of distributing value created by a corporation to its stakeholders, including shareholders, workers, managers, and banks. Institutional shareholders, one of those value extractors, have limited liabilities over the corporations and are legally protected from corporate failures, not more than the loss of their shareholding. They are, therefore, not directly involved in management and only voice their requests or concerns to management through directors or shareholder meetings.

5.1.1 Does Stronger Activism Lead to Better Value Creation?

In understanding the relationship between value creation and value extraction, an important fact is that institutional shareholders' professional capability primarily lies in portfolio management, which includes stock-picking, market timing, and tracking stock-price movements. These stock-trading capabilities are very different from the managerial capabilities required for value creation. Coffee (2012) confirms these characteristics in his interviews, "institutional investors regularly stress that they are stock traders and portfolio managers, not management consultants" (p. 495).

Most institutional shareholders also lack ability and interest in monitoring their portfolio companies sufficiently closely to enable them to contribute to the value-creation process, as such monitoring would require substantial cost and the acquisition of capabilities to comprehend the value-creation process that, by their training, they do not have.[135] As will be discussed in Section 5.2. in detail, institutional shareholders have, in fact, become less interested in and less capable of closely monitoring their portfolio companies.

Without explaining how the value creation process is connected to value extraction, shareholder activism has progressed with the economic rhetoric that stronger activism and more involvement in management by public shareholders would improve value creation in corporations. But the rhetoric was only theoretically supported by AT-MSV. One reason AT-MSV posits that the rhetoric is the reality has to do with its assumption of the market equilibrium in the

---

[134] For details about value creation by corporations, refer to Lazonick and Shin (2020, Chapters 1 & 2); Lazonick (2023, Chapter 2).

[135] For details about value extraction by shareholders and the stock market, refer to Lazonick and Shin (2020, Chapters 1 & 3); Lazonick (2023, Chapters 3 & 4).

beginning. Following the Neoclassical economics tradition, AT-MSV theorists start their analyses from a world of equilibrium where there is no market distortion.[136] They then add one distortion to this model: the agency cost incurred by managers. It is only natural that, in this idealized world with only one distortion, removing it by shareholder activism will make the economy return to equilibrium.

However, the neoclassical equilibrium they suppose as an ideal state is, in fact, the state where there is no innovation. Innovation is a process of overcoming uncertainties, and corporate value is created as a result. But there is no uncertainty to overcome in an equilibrium state and hence no innovation. Schumpeter (1934) describes this situation as "circular flow" and emphasizes that innovation, that is, "New Combinations" happens by breaking the circular flow, that is, the flow of old combinations. Lazonick (2022) also points out that a firm operating in the neoclassical equilibrium is in fact the "most unproductive firm" and ironically becomes the foundation of the most "efficient" economy in the neoclassical analysis. Returning to equilibrium by removing supposed agency costs has nothing to do with innovation and value creation.

Even in the real world, where agency costs negatively affect the operating performance of a company, simply reducing them does not necessarily improve the performance. A company needs to reduce the total cost, not merely agency costs. Even if some agency costs remain, it will choose a way to lower the overall costs if the outcome is better than that of reducing agency costs only. The impact of agency costs is only a part of the operational performance in the real world, and there is no guarantee that it outweighs all the other components affecting the performance.

5.1.2 The Fallacy of AT-MSV's "Residual Claimants" Argument

Another critical flaw of AT-MSV lies in its contention that shareholders are the only "residual claimants" who do not have "guaranteed returns." The "residual claimants" argument elevates the status of public shareholders to owners of the corporation who bear the highest risk, on the one hand, and provides the justification that corporations should run for their maximum benefit (even at the expense of other participants in the corporation), on the other. Let me deal with the issue of residual claims in the real world first and the ownership issue later.

Contrary to agency theorists' claim, shareholders are not the only corporate participants who bear risk. Taxpayers and workers also make risky investments

---

[136] Refer to Jensen and Meckling (1976); Fama (1980); Fama and Jensen (1983); Jensen (1986, 1988, 1993); Jensen and Murphy (1990).

in productive capabilities on a regular basis. Through government investments and subsidies, taxpayers regularly provide productive resources to companies without a guaranteed return. Through the tax system, governments, representing taxpayers in general, seek to extract this return from corporations and individuals that reap the rewards of government spending. Through the political process, however, tax rates and revenues are subject to change, and hence the returns to taxpayers are by no means guaranteed.

Workers also regularly make productive contributions to the companies for which they work through the exercise of skill and effort beyond those levels required to lay claim to their current pay, but without guaranteed returns. Any employer who is seeking to generate higher quality and lower cost products knows the profound productivity difference between employees who just punch the clock to get their daily pay and those who engage in learning to make productive contributions through which they can build their careers and thereby reap future returns in work and in retirement. Yet these careers and the returns that they can generate are not guaranteed.

From this perspective, both the state and labor have "residual claimants" status; that is, an economic claim on the distribution of profits, if and when they occur. AT-MSV ignores the risk-reward relation for these two types of economic actors in the operation and performance of business corporations. Moreover, public shareholders do not, as a rule, invest directly in the corporation. Rather, once a firm is publicly listed, households or asset managers become shareholders by purchasing shares outstanding on the stock market. They enjoy limited liability while they hold the shares and, given the liquidity of the stock market, at any instant and at a very low transaction cost they can take a "Wall Street Walk," that is, sell the shares at the going market price and dissociate themselves from the companies whose shares they used to own. When financiers such as venture capitalists make equity investments in a start-up in the absence of a liquid market for the company's shares, they are residual claimants because they contribute to the company's value-creating capabilities and face the risk that the firm will not be able to generate a return or even go bankrupt. In the stock market, financiers' investments in new stock issues are very small compared to their trading of old shares. Public shareholders are, in general, value extractors, not value creators. Without examining the actual risk-taking in the value creation process, AT-MSV elevates public shareholders to the status of the only risk bearers.[137]

---

[137] Discussion here is from Lazonick and Shin (2020, pp. 65–66); Lazonick (2023, pp. 45–49).

5.1.3 Business-Managing Fiduciary vs. Money-Managing Fiduciary

AT-MSV's claims that corporate managers are agents of shareholders because shareholders "own" corporations are also not justifiable from the legal perspective of incorporation. Once a firm is incorporated, all its assets are owned by the corporation, that is, the legal entity specifically set up to manage the assets and conduct businesses, founders turn into shareholders, owners of shares issued by the corporation, not owners of the corporation. Jean-Philippe Robé (2011), a legal scholar and practitioner, calls this "the first separation of ownership and control" in contrast to "the second separation of ownership and control" described by Berle and Means (1932) about the emergence of large public corporations with dispersed shareholding in the US in the early twentieth century.

I would put Robé's "first separation" as the "permanent separation of ownership and control." The "permanent separation" or "first separation" occurs at the time of incorporation, and this process is well-established in the legal profession, with different names such as "capital lock-in," "affirmative asset partitioning," "asset separation from shareholders," and "the absence of a repurchase condition."[138] There is hardly any dispute about this permanent separation when a company is incorporated. The ownership is separated from founders who, in return for transferring their assets to the corporation, become shareholders with controlling rights and monetary rights over the corporation. Even in a corporation with only one shareholder, the person does not own it. He or she has 100 percent control over the corporation.

Confusion arises with terms such as Berle and Means' "separation of ownership and control" or Robé's "second separation of ownership and control." What these terms indicate is the "dispersion of control." In US corporations set up in the nineteenth century, the separation between ownership and control already happened as soon as they were incorporated. Since then, corporations have owned themselves all the while, that is, there was no more separation of ownership and control. What happened later in the late nineteenth century and early twentieth century in some large US corporations was that the control passed from their founding shareholders to professional managers, as Figure 7 shows. When founding shareholders sold their shares in the market and retired from management, institutional shareholders hardly existed, and it was mainly individuals who purchased the shares. These retail shareholders were weak and dispersed. They were only interested in the monetary rights attached to their shares, that is, prospective dividends and capital gains. They had neither the will nor the collective power to exercise the controlling rights coming with the

---

[138] Stout (2013); Blair (2003b); Hansmann and Kraakman (2000); Klein and Coffee (2004); Demsetz (1995); Robé (2011).

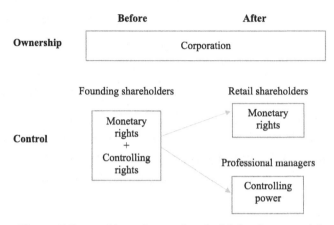

Figure 7 Ownership and control at the birth of managerial capitalism in the US

shares they owned. Hence, the control was passed to professional managers who had worked with the founders and stayed true to their founding spirits by continuing to invest for the long term. The US thus entered the era of "managerial capitalism" with this dispersion of control in large corporations.[139] Robé's "second separation" is also not correct because the ownership has already separated, and there was no ownership to be separated again.

Understanding the process of incorporation is important to understanding for whom managers work. AT-MSV insists that managers are agents of shareholders only by relying on the untenable "residual claimants" argument. As a result of the permanent separation, however, shareholders do not own the corporation or its assets. They have become owners of special securities, that is, shares, issued by the corporation and are entitled to controlling and monetary rights over the corporation. They can exert their controlling rights through the board of directors or shareholder meetings. Robé (2011) thus emphasizes, "The shareholders enjoy the privileges of the owner towards what they own: the shares. They don't and can't have these privileges towards the corporation having issued the shares" (p. 3).

Due to this permanent separation of ownership and control, shareholders do not enter employment contracts. As an independent legal person, a corporation makes employment contracts with its managers. Managers are, therefore, agents of the corporation, not shareholders. They serve the corporation for its survival and prosperity. In other words, corporate managers are "business-managing

---

[139] On managerial capitalism, refer to Lazonick (1991, 1992, 2007); Chandler (1962, 1977, 1990); Lazonick and O'Sullivan (2000).

fiduciaries" entrusted by the corporation. Ignoring this fundamental relationship between the corporation and its shareholders and bypassing the existence of the corporation, AT-MSV connects shareholders and managers directly and places managers as agents of shareholders.

Monks and other shareholder activists even attempt to elevate institutional shareholders to the status of corporations' "owners." It is not frequent that institutional shareholders portray themselves as "owners."[140] However, they do not own shares of corporations with their own money. They are managing money that savers put in their custody. In other words, institutional shareholders are "money-managing fiduciaries" entrusted by savers. So, the relationship between corporate managers and institutional shareholders is not vertical, contrary to what institutional activists purport. It is a horizontal one between two different fiduciaries serving different customers. There should be constructive conversations between the two fiduciaries, not an order from one fiduciary to another.

5.2 Uninterested and Incapable, but Strong Institutional Shareholders

Shareholder activism also went astray because characteristics of institutional shareholding have evolved far away from the ideal of shareholder democracy. Shareholder activists maintained the outdated outlook of "dispersed ownership" and portrayed institutional shareholders as weak "minority shareholders" who did not have effective means of voicing their concerns to "all-powerful" corporate management. They then sought to strengthen the power of institutional shareholders against management by changing regulations so that they could easily aggregate their voting power by allowing de facto investor cartels with "free communication and engagement."

However, institutional shareholding already surpassed 40 percent of all shares outstanding in 1980 and approached 52 percent in 1990, making institutional shareholders the most dominant corporate shareholders (Figure 1). Moreover, institutional shareholding has been extremely concentrated in the hands of relatively few large institutional shareholders. For example, in 2022, the ten largest institutional shareholders held stock valued at $22.3 trillion, nearly 60 percent of that held by the 100 largest institutional shareholders, as Table 1 shows. Even among these ten largest institutional shareholders, concentration is remarkable. The "Big Three," (BlackRock, Vanguard, and State Street) held $13.3 trillion of stock, more than one-third (35.4 percent) of public shares held by the 100 largest

---

[140] For instance, The Stern School of Business at New York University (NYU) organized "Institutional Investors as Owners Conference" in 2005, and major institutional shareholders took part in it (Biggs 2005).

Table 1 The concentration of shareholding among institutional
shareholders (2022)

Rank	Institutional Shareholders	Shareholdings ($ billion)
1	Vanguard Group, Inc.	5,968
2	BlackRock, Inc.	5,193
3	The Capital Group Companies, Inc	2,181
4	State Street Corporation	2,168
5	Fidelity Investments	1,982
6	T. Rowe Price Group, Inc.	1,151
7	Geode Capital Management, LLC	995
8	JPMorgan Chase & Co.	917
9	Bank of America Corporation	844
10	UBS Group AG	776
	The "Big Three"	13,343 (35.4%)
	Top 5 Holders	17,494 (46.4%)
	Top 10 Holders	22,179 (58.8%)
	Top 25 Holders	29,405 (78%)
	Top 100 Holders	37,705 (100%)

Source: Refinitiv Eikon database compiled by Emre Gömec of The Academic-Industry Research Network and University of Kassel (September 2023).

institutional shareholders. They "collectively vote about 20% of the shares in all S&P 500 companies" in 2018.[141] The US stock market is dominated by a few institutional shareholders, the "King Kong of investment America," as the Vanguard founder John Bogle pointed out.[142] Their power is greater and more concentrated than that of large corporations.

In the conventional characterization of "dispersed ownership," public shareholders, including institutional shareholders, are described as powerless "minority shareholders" who have no means to influence the management. "King Kong" institutional shareholders, however, amassed unprecedented voting power over individual companies. For instance, As Table 2 shows, BlackRock held 5 percent or more of the outstanding shares in 3,157 companies in 2022. Vanguard and Fidelity held 5 percent or more of the shares in 2,234 companies and 992 companies, respectively. In an article entitled "The Giant of Shareholders, Quietly Stirring," the New York Times reported in 2013 that BlackRock was "the single largest shareholder in one of every five U.S. companies including Exxon Mobil and Chevron; AT&T and Verizon; JPMorgan Chase

---

[141] Bebchuk and Hirst (2019).   [142] Bogle (2005).

Table 2 Number of companies in which an institutional shareholder
has a 5 percent or greater stake (2022)

Institutional shareholder	Number of global companies
BlackRock, Inc.	3,157
Vanguard Group, Inc.	2,234
Fidelity Investments	992
Capital Group Companies, Inc.	446
State Street Corporation	432
T. Rowe Price Group, Inc.	337
JPMorgan Chase & Co.	123
UBS Group AG	45
Bank of America Corporation	18
Geode Capital Management, LLC	3

Source: Refinitiv Eikon database compiled by Emre Gömec of The Academic-Industry Research Network and University of Kassel (September 2023).

and Citigroup; GE; and more than 800 others. It also holds 5% or more shares of 1,803 U.S.-listed companies, about 40% of U.S.-listed companies."[143]

Their voting power over individual companies is more remarkable when we consider the fact that these largest institutional shareholders are the most diversified stock traders in world history. Leading mutual funds and pension funds rely heavily on holdings in index funds such as exchange-traded funds (ETFs), by which they effectively "own the market," as the number of portfolio companies in a fund sometimes exceeds 10,000. Even though their portfolios are often criticized for "excessive diversification," they are still the single largest shareholders in a great number of public companies.

A serious problem with the voting power of index funds lies in the fact that they are neither interested in nor capable of voting even if they have already become the most important and powerful shareholders of US public corporations. John C. Coates (2018), a professor at Harvard Law School and formally an acting director of the SEC's division of corporation finance, estimated in 2018 that "indexed funds now own more than 20% and perhaps 30% or more of nearly all U.S. public companies."[144] The wide variation of his estimates is understandable. Firstly, official statistics on index funds released by Investment Company Institute only include "registered index fund assets." Yet a large and increasing portion of assets held by pension funds, insurance companies and non-profits are managed in index fashion. Secondly, the statistics do not include

---

[143] Craig (2013).   [144] Coates (2018, p. 13).

foreign funds. Foreign funds hold about 20 percent of all US equities, and they are managed in index fashion much more than domestic funds.[145] Thirdly, a large portion of "nominally active funds" are in fact managed in index fashion.[146] Whether one chooses to use the lower bound or the higher bound of the estimates, the dominance of index funds in the shareholding of US public corporations is likely to be strengthened further for quite a long while. Coates projected: "If current growth rates continued . . ., the entire U.S. market would be held by such funds no later than 2030. But even if the trend flattens, the majority of most companies will soon be owned by indexed funds."[147]

Index funds' critical competitive edge lies in the extremely low fees they charge to customers. They do so by managing funds through tracking indexes rather than picking shares of individual companies. They track indexes mostly with computer models by compiling information on companies and markets that is publicly available. They also enjoy greater economies of scale than active funds because, once an indexation model is devised, it is easily replicable in other funds with only minimum revisions and extra costs. They do not need to spend money and time to research individual companies in an attempt to find additional information unique to those companies. Unlike active funds that enjoy a decisive competitive edge due to such information, being uninterested in individual companies and remaining incapable of knowing about their unique information is the *raison d'être* of index funds.

Related to the growth of index funds, the portion of assets managed by artificial intelligence (AI) has increased dramatically. On the New York Stock Exchange, high-frequency trading (HFT) accounted for over half of the total trading volume after peaking at over 60 percent in 2009 (Figure 8). As a result, the average stock holding period was shortened from 57.1 months in 1980 to 15.4 months in 2000, and 4.8 months in 2009.[148] The financial market is flooded with reports such as "Algorithms Take Control of Wall Street," "A.I. Controls the Stock Market," "The U.S. Stock Market Belongs to Bots."[149] A JPMorgan

---

[145] Coates (2018, p. 11) explains this as follows: "Much of that ownership is indexed. While precise data on how much are not available, it is fair to assume that a greater portion of foreign ownership is truly passive than is the case for domestic. That is because foreign investors have good reasons to understand that their knowledge of foreign markets will tend to be worse than for domestic investors, and so attempting to out-guess the markets through market timing or picking stocks will fail."

[146] Coates (2018, p. 11) elaborates on this as follows: "Active funds commonly minimize management costs by essentially holding an index and selecting a few companies to over- or under-weight. This allows them to distinguish themselves from the index funds, while not attempting to engage in serious analysis of the value of each portfolio company. The "active share," as the portion of active funds that is significantly different from what would follow from a passive indexing strategy is commonly estimated to exceed 50 percent at many funds, resulting in an additional chunk of the market being fairly understood as indexed and truly passive."

[147] Coates (2018, p. 13).   [148] Wong (2010).

[149] Salmon and Stokes (2010); Danneman (2017); Burger (2017).

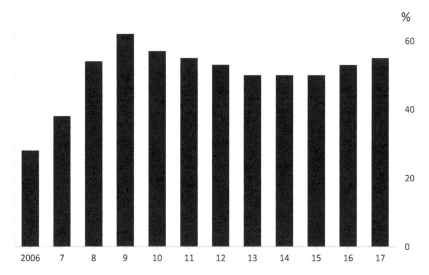

Figure 8 HFT as a share of US equities daily volume
Source: Meyer et al. (2018).

Chase report estimated that discretionary equity trading accounts for only about 10 percent of the total trading after removing HFT and index fund trading.[150] It is impossible to expect that these AIs would behave as responsible and capable "corporate citizens."

This change in the shareholding and trading structure reveals the schizophrenia of shareholder activists. In their zeal for activism, they envisioned a new world where institutional shareholders become more active and capable of intervening in corporate management through "relational investing." However, institutional shareholders have evolved toward being less interested and less capable in proxy voting and engagement. Ironically, the legitimacy of institutional shareholders' proxy voting and engagement has eroded as their power over corporations has increased. In denial of this new reality and, at the same time, sensing and exploiting the growing power of institutional shareholders, shareholder activists have only pressed for strengthening activism by aggregating power of already powerful institutional shareholders.

5.3 Misguided Compulsory Voting: Power to Proxy Advisory Firms

Monks invoked the concept of "citizenship" from political democracy when he pushed for compulsory voting of institutional shareholders. Like him, advocates of shareholder democracy have tended to employ analogies taken from political

---

[150] Quoted in Burger (2017).

democracy. But Monks critically erred in using this analogy because compulsory voting is not a norm of political elections in most countries. He did not examine why it is not so or what its implications are for shareholder democracy. More importantly, he avoided assessing what real effects imposing compulsory voting as a fiduciary duty would have on the behavior of institutional shareholders.

5.3.1 Incorrect and Arbitrary Analogy to Political Voting

In a political election, compulsory voting certainly has its pros and cons. It can have the positive effect of augmenting the power of representation by increasing the turnout of voters at the ballot box. However, it can have negative effects on an election outcome because it increases blank, randomly marked, and spoilt ballots from voters who are not interested in the election and do not know about the candidates. These uninterested voters are also more prone to cast their votes in response to hot-button issues of the day or political scandals, rather than trying to align their voting with ideological or policy preferences.[151]

The political reality around the world is that, whatever the theoretical balance of pros and cons, only a small number of countries adopt a compulsory voting system. There were 22 out of about 200 countries in 2019, including Australia, Brazil, and Singapore, where compulsory national voting was in effect and two local governments that had made voting compulsory.[152] Most countries consider voting as a right, not as a duty that they should enforce on their citizens. Many countries also take the position that abstaining from voting is also an expression of political preference that should be allowed in accordance with the constitutional right of freedom of speech. The fact that most countries do not adopt compulsory voting in political elections tells us that they are much more concerned with its cons than with its pros.

Yet advocates of compulsory voting for institutional shareholders presented only its potential pros, without considering or presenting either its cons or what the net effect of those pros and cons would be. If one looks into the nature and process of proxy voting by institutional shareholders, it is not hard to find that the cons of compulsory proxy voting are a lot more pronounced than those of compulsory political voting. In a political election, the secret ballot is the norm: Voters are guaranteed the secrecy of their ballots and not compelled to explain their voting decisions. In this situation, the negative effects of voting at random can be mitigated by the law of large numbers. In proxy voting, however, institutional shareholders are required not only to declare how they voted but

---

[151] Refer to Birch (2009); Brennan and Hil (2014); Singh (2015); Lever (2010); Volacu (2020).

[152] "Countries that have mandatory voting," *Stacker* (September 13, 2019), https://stacker.com/stories/3485/countries-have-mandatory-voting.

also to provide justification for their voting decisions.[153] Therefore, uninterested institutional shareholders are compelled to create or purchase justifications for their voting decisions. Even those who are interested in voting may decide to vote against their own preferences if strong public backlash against their voting decisions appears likely when they reveal their voting decisions.

Moreover, proxy voting is wide open to conflicts of interest whereas there is no room for conflict of interests in political voting (unless one can divide a person). In fact, the phenomenal growth of both the stock market and institutional investment has greatly lengthened and complicated the chain of intermediaries involved in institutional shareholding. In pension-fund investments, for instance, the chain extends from pensioners to pension administrators, pension investment advisers, funds of funds, external asset managers, and others. The relation among those intermediaries has also become very complex because, even within one mutual fund, there are numerous sub-funds (Figure 9). Considering the length and

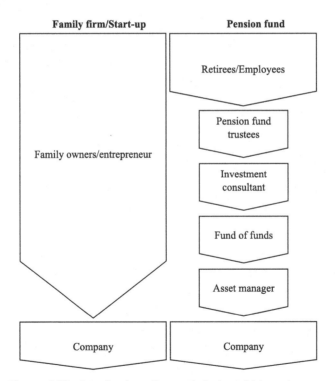

Figure 9 The lengthening of control chains within and among institutional shareholders

Source: Wong (2010)

---

[153] 17 C.F.R. §§ 275.206(4)-6 (2021).

complexity of this chain, it is questionable whether those at the end of the chain would really exercise voting rights over corporations on behalf of the customers who had put money into their custody. Far detached from the original customers, institutional shareholders may cast their votes in their own interest rather than in the interest of those whose proxies they hold.

This possibility of conflicts of interest becomes greater if the original customers have little power to replace their intermediaries, as typically is the case with public pension funds. Putting it in the terminology of agency theorists, institutional shareholders are prone to their own agency problems when they cast their votes ostensibly in attempts to resolve agency problems of corporate managers. These conflicts of interest were already evident as the empirical research on institutional activism detailed in Section 4.1 shows.

Nonetheless, the SEC expressed naïve expectations about the benefits of compulsory proxy voting in the "Final rule" in 2003, and this stance has not changed so far:

> "Although we recognize that compliance programs, including proxy voting programs, may require advisers to expend resources that they could otherwise use in their primary business, we expect that the rules and rule amendments may indirectly increase efficiency in a number of ways. Advisers would be required to carry out their proxy voting in an organized and systematic manner, which may be more efficient than their current approach. Requiring all advisers with voting authority to adopt proxy voting policies and procedures, and meet recordkeeping requirements, may enhance efficiency further by encouraging third parties to create new resources and guidance to which industry participants can refer in establishing, improving, and implementing their proxy voting procedures."[154]

The SEC's position is based on the optimistic expectation that institutional shareholders would develop analytic capabilities to make voting decisions "in an organized and systematic manner," and that "third parties" would be competent and objective in providing advice. Reality has shown this optimism to have been unfounded. Far from taking compliance seriously, the largest institutional shareholders, especially index funds, have limited their efforts to setting up skeletal research units that barely paid lip service to the new rule. Nor have the "third parties," the proxy-advisory firms, equipped themselves adequately for their task; still, they exert undue power over the voting decisions of institutional shareholders and, thereby over corporations. In addition, they also have a serious potential for conflict of interest, as will be detailed below.

---

[154] 17 C.F.R. §§ 275.206(4)-6 (2021); SEC (2003).

5.3.2 "Corporate-Governance Teams": Lip-Service Voting Organizations of Large Institutional Shareholders

Most large mutual funds had rarely taken part in corporate voting before it became compulsory in 2003. That was a natural and, in my view, appropriate position, considering the fact that the larger portion of their assets was held in index funds. Simply tracking index movements rather than researching individual companies constitutes the critical competitive edge that has enabled mutual funds to charge very low management fees and, consequently, to increase their AUM rapidly.

When the SEC ruled proxy voting to be among their fiduciary duties, the mutual funds initially relied heavily on recommendations from proxy-advisory firms; in other words, they "purchased" proxy-voting decisions and related justifications. However, criticisms soon emerged of both this practice and the proxy-advisory firms. Large mutual funds were, therefore, under pressure to demonstrate to policymakers, their own customers, and the public that they were dutifully fulfilling this new fiduciary obligation. Many of them then adopted the two-pronged approach of separating the voting decisions of the active funds and passive funds under their management and setting up a corporate governance team or stewardship team for the latter.

BlackRock offers an illuminating case in this regard. It divides its voting decisions between active-management funds and passive-management funds. The proxy decisions of the former are made primarily by the fund managers in charge of the portfolio firms concerned. In contrast, the proxy decisions of the latter are under the control of its Corporate Governance Team, whose name was later changed to Stewardship Team.[155] To outsiders, this team is portrayed as being equipped to make informed voting decisions and to engage professionally with portfolio companies. The reality, however, lies far from this rosy picture. In the 2012 proxy season, the team consisting of only 20 people voted on 129,814 proposals at 14,872 shareholder meetings worldwide.[156] BlackRock steadily increased the number of its stewardship team members to over 70 and voted on 173,326 proposals at 18,272 shareholder meetings in 2022. One person dealt with 2,476 proxy votes in 261 shareholder meetings annually.[157] The only feasible way to deal with so many voting decisions with such limited personnel is to apply some general corporate-governance metrics rather than to examine the concrete contexts of individual companies' voting issues.

---

[155] Other largest institutional investors maintain the similar structure of dividing voting decisions between passive funds and active funds.

[156] Loomis (2014).

[157] 'BlackRock Investment Stewardship 2022 Annual Report,' www.blackrock.com/corporate/literature/publication/annual-stewardship-report-2022.pdf (Accessed on January 17, 2024).

The *New York Times* thus described the team's decision-making as "the corporate governance equivalent of speed dating" and reported as follows: "These analysts have a language of their own, casually throwing around terms like 'overboarding,' for when directors serve on multiple boards, possibly spreading themselves too thin; 'engagement,' when a problem reaches a critical stage and merits a visit from a BlackRock analyst; and 'refreshment', when engagement doesn't work and a director needs a heaveho."[158]

The situation of the other largest institutional shareholders is not different from that of BlackRock. Dorothy S. Lund (2018) reports, "Vanguard employs fifteen people devoted to engagement and voting at about 13,000 companies based around the world ... and State Street employs fewer than ten people devoted to governance issues at around 9,000 companies. Put differently, each member of Vanguard's governance team is tasked with making governance decisions for nearly one thousand companies, even though Vanguard is likely to be one of the company's largest shareholders."[159]

This reality only reinforces the suspicion that minimizing the size of the corporate governance team is an inexpensive and likely the only option for the largest index funds to demonstrate to the regulators and public that they carry out the fiduciary duty of proxy voting. In this sense, one may say that corporate governance teams are "lip-service" units that have resulted from the imposition of compulsory voting on institutional shareholders.

Nonetheless, this kind of lip-service proxy voting significantly affects the actual outcome of proxy contests. Above all, some institutional shareholders are very powerful individually and have already become the largest shareholders in numerous companies, as mentioned in Section 5.2. Moreover, the voting decisions are implicitly coordinated among institutional shareholders because they employ similar metrics, even if they may not explicitly collude with each other. For instance, Lund (2018) mentions:

> "In spite of the fact that there are no generally accepted best practices for governance, the Big Three have adopted nearly identical voting guidelines: each institution articulates a preference for director independence; some relationship between long-term company performance and executive compensation; and skepticism about anti-takeover provisions and major changes to the corporation, such as mergers, reorganizations, or changes to capital structure" (p. 516).

This potential collusion is likely because corporate governance teams in those institutional shareholders tend to employ a similar set of corporate governance metrics. Institutional shareholders are also increasingly under public pressure to make their "voting policies" explicit and they tend to put up their policy

---

[158] Craig (2013).   [159] Lund (2018, p. 516).

statements on voting and engagements. It is then highly probable that institutional shareholders take others' policy statements and previous voting decisions on similar cases into their voting decisions. "No explicit collusion is required to send highly aligned signals about what they want to each other and to management of portfolio companies," as Coates (2018, p. 15) points out.

5.3.3 ISS, the Proxy-Voting Monster: Its Inadequacy and Illegitimate Power

Only the largest index funds have the financial resources to set up in-house corporate governance teams. For the other smaller index funds, the most convenient and feasible way to fulfill their fiduciary duty is to follow proxy-advisory firms' recommendations. Even large institutional shareholders rely heavily on proxy-advisory firms in the actual working of their corporate-governance teams. According to Charles M. Nathan (2010),

> "Many investment managers have chosen a hybrid model ... For example, they may utilize some or all of the services offered by proxy advisory firms, including voting recommendation services, but rely on the institution's internal corporate governance staff for final voting decisions on some or all ballot issues. Other institutions use internal staff for administrative functions but as a matter of formal policy or informal practice follow the voting recommendations of third-party proxy advisors" (p. 19).[160]

On a closer look, the abilities of proxy-advisory firms are hardly more impressive than those of the corporate-governance teams. As of 2017, ISS controlled 63 percent of the proxy-advisory market, while Glass Lewis and Co. controlled 28 percent, together creating a duopoly in the market.[161] ISS is unmatched in its influence over large institutional shareholders, claiming to advise "24 out of the top 25" mutual funds and "17 out of the top 25" pension funds.[162] Considering its dominance in the proxy-advisory market, focusing exclusively on the case of ISS will suffice for this Element.

Although ISS only had 1,100 employees, including its administrative staff, it recommended yes-or-no decisions on more than 9.6 million ballots representing 3.7 trillion shares a year in 115 countries in 2018.[163] How could it have developed the capacity and expertise to make so many voting decisions on such diverse issues in so many companies? After all, company management and

---

[160] Nathan (2010).   [161] Shu (2020).   [162] Rose (2007).

[163] The ISS website, at https://www.issgovernance.com/about/about-iss/ (visited on November 20, 2018). In January 2014, when I visited the same website, ISS no longer provided the number of ballots it exercises annually and only said, "ISS' 3,000 employees operate worldwide across 25 global locations in 15 countries. Its approximately 3,400 clients ... " (accessed on January 17, 2024).

shareholders often bring controversial proposals to shareholder meetings. It may not be that difficult – although time-consuming – to draft a well-reasoned report comparing the pros and cons of a proposal. However, it is very difficult to express clear approval or disapproval. It strains credulity to think that ISS, with so few employees, developed the complex, high-level expertise capable of making authoritative recommendations on so many issues worldwide.[164] With the constraints of a limited workforce, the only option for ISS is to apply general and mechanical corporate-governance metrics to its voting recommendations, just as the largest index funds' corporate-governance teams tend to do. In this context, Nathan (2010) mentions as follows:

> "The proxy advisory firms' methodology for recommending voting positions in a manner intended to satisfy the fiduciary prudent man standard consists of an increasingly complex set of voting policies designed to cover every vote on every shareholder meeting ballot. Application of those policies is routinized and implemented by a combination of computer systems and a low cost labor source that has the capability of linking the voting policies to the actual ballot issues, as presented in each company's proxy materials" (p, 19).[165]

In reality, ISS tends to apply general and mechanical corporate-governance metrics to its voting recommendations, just as the largest index funds' corporate-governance teams tend to do. Because of this lip-servicing function of ISS, institutional shareholders, its major customers, did not care about or rely upon ISS before they were required to vote. Indeed, ISS, the only proxy-advisory firm at the time, was struggling to stay in business. Its business took off only when its "lip service" became necessary for mutual funds with the SEC's final rule on proxy voting in 2003.[166]

For most index funds, just following the recommendations of proxy-advisory firms is the most convenient way to fulfill their fiduciary duty "because they can't justify to shareholders why they invest in their own analysis."[167] Only the largest index funds, such as BlackRock and Vanguards, set up in-house corporate-governance teams. Lesser index funds have no alternative but to rely heavily on proxy firms' advice. Even many active funds tend to follow the recommendations of proxy-advisory firms; combing through proxy firms' analyses and voting recommendations is a normal first step for fund managers.

---

[164] The situation in Glass Lewis is even worse. The second-largest proxy advisory firm states on its website that it has "more than 380 employees worldwide, more than half of whom are dedicated to research," cover "more than 30,000 meetings each year, across approximately 100 global markets." 'Company Overview,' Glass Lewis website at http://www.glasslewis.com/company-overview/ (last visited January 16, 2024).

[165] Also refer to Rose (2007, p. 907–913).　　[166] Refer to Section 3.2.

[167] Bew and Fields (2012, p. 15).

In addition, an internal convention at most institutional shareholders dictates that, if fund managers want to go against proxy firms' recommendations, they provide a lengthy report to their superiors to justify their decisions – something they don't need to do if they simply go along with the recommendations. Going against proxy firms' recommendations thus requires courage and effort on the part of fund managers who are busy attempting to make profitable trades for the portfolios they manage. In this respect, the root of the power and influence of ISS is not really the quality of its work, but rather the convenience it provides to institutional shareholders by lightening the burden of performing the unwanted obligation of voting proxies.

Moreover, proxy firms are wide open to conflict of interest because, as unregulated private business entities, they are responsible to nobody except their own businesses. They normally combine proxy-voting advisory services with consulting services. When there is a proxy contest between one of their customers and a non-customer, it is hardly difficult for them to side with their customer, packaging their support as an "objective" assessment. As private and unregulated entities, there is no way for outsiders to determine whether the voting recommendations of the proxy firms were made objectively or shaped to serve their own business interests.

There is also a tendency for proxy firms to provide voting advice that reflects the investment philosophy of their owners. Set up by corporate-governance activist Robert Monks, ISS would be likely to side with an activist fund in a controversy pitting such a fund against company management. The ownership of ISS was later transferred to Vestar Capital, a private-equity fund that was founded by corporate raiders from First Boston's leveraged-buyout team, and then in 2017 to Genstar Capital, another private-equity fund. It would be only natural for ISS to support activist hedge funds when they have proxy battles with industrial companies.

In effect, compulsory voting for institutional shareholders has given ISS illegitimate power. Officially, it is only an "advisory" firm lacking any legitimate basis whatsoever for exerting influence on corporate decisions of the kind that must be approved in shareholder meetings. However, one cannot ignore its influence: A negative recommendation by ISS on a management proposal has been found to reduce the support of institutional shareholders by at least 13.6 percent and, at most, by 20.6 percent.[168] Corporate executives have to

---

[168] Bethel and Gillan (2002, p. 30). Shu (2021) reports a similar result, "[W]hen ISS recommends against a particular director's election, its customers are 21 percent more likely than other investors to vote against this director ... The same pattern also applies for nonbinding advisory votes on executive compensation ("Say on Pay"), wherein ISS ... can sway 20 percent ... of their customers' votes" (pp. 2–3).

take a two-digit percentage difference very seriously, as it is often the case that the eventual voting outcome is decided by a thin margin. Iliev and Lowry (2015) reported that over 25 percent of mutual funds "almost entirely" rely on ISS recommendations when they cast votes. A Business Roundtable survey found that 40 percent of its member firms' shares were held by institutions that basically followed ISS's voting recommendations.[169]

ISS's influence becomes stronger because it also coordinates with institutional shareholders in making those recommendations. As Coffee and Palia (2016) remark, "[ISS and Glass Lewis] . . . determine their voting policies based on interactions with (and polling of) institutional shareholders, so that proxy advisors and their clients reciprocally influence each other" (p. 558). It is therefore not an exaggeration to say that "[powerful] CEOs come on bended knees to ISS to persuade the managers of ISS of the merits of their views."[170]

The illegitimate power of proxy firms arose partly because the proxy-advisory market is basically a duopoly and because, even between its two members, ISS is easily the dominant one. If there were a number of proxy-advisory firms with similar reputations and if institutional shareholders could choose from among their diverse recommendations, their service might be defined as – and confined to – "advice". However, when the imposition of compulsory voting made it necessary to fill the vacuum of institutional votes that had previously existed, the larger part of this job fell to ISS, upon which nobody had conferred legitimate power to influence voting decisions in the corporate arena. ISS is a monster created by compulsory voting. No corporation anywhere in the world sends ISS a formal invitation to take part in its shareholders' meeting. But it effectively attends these meetings and casts votes, and nobody dares to expel ISS for exercising illegitimate influence on voting outcomes of the meeting.

5.4 Consequences of "Free Communication and Engagement"

In bringing about the 1992 proxy-rule amendments, shareholder activists employed an analogy from political democracy. They portrayed corporate management as autocrats who ignored popular demands for freedom of speech and freedom of assembly while installing strict censorship in the form of proxy-filing procedures that, they charged, unfairly favored management. In contrast, they portrayed themselves as endeavoring to realize a true shareholder democracy by abolishing the censorship and thus obtaining the right of free communication and engagement. They then justified the proxy-rule changes by arguing

---

[169] Briggs (2007, p. 692).

[170] Strine (2005, p. 688). For detailed accounts of how ISS and other proxy advisory firms actually influenced voting outcomes and how they interacted with hedge-fund activists in major proxy battles, refer to Walker (2016).

that they would correct the imbalance between shareholders and management and bring about a more efficient market outcome.

However, such expectations are based on the critical assumption that freer and easier exchange of information has an efficiency-enhancing effect in the market, an assumption that follows from conventional economic models of competitive markets, which are in turn based on the assumption that interaction among players who have equal capability and equal access to information is the key to ensuring an efficient outcome. But markets in general, and the stock market in particular, do not function according to this neoclassical model. Markets may be unduly influenced by strong movers and shakers, and the stock market in particular is prone to manipulation. As it turned out, the very practices that the traditional regulations were meant to deter by preventing free communication and engagement, "fraud or deceit" and "manipulative or deceptive devices or contrivances", became more widespread because of the proxy-rule changes and compulsory proxy voting.[171]

The "wolf-pack phenomenon" – sudden concerted campaigns of hedge funds against their target companies – has become a new normal since the 1992 proxy-rule changes.[172] Wolf packs can only be seen as *de facto* investor cartels. In conventional economics, cartels are considered prime obstacles to realizing the efficient allocation of resources, and they are therefore regulated heavily in most countries with capitalist economies. The existence of unregulated wolf packs is testament to the fact that, with the proxy-rule changes the SEC effectively gave up its duty as a market regulator, employing the rhetoric of promoting "market efficiency" to hide this failure.

The SEC might have naively thought that freely allowing investor cartels made up of shareholders, none of which held less than 5 percent of the target company's stock, would not undermine "market efficiency". However, in light of the broad dispersion of shareholding in big public companies, those with a 5 percent stake can easily exert a strong influence on management. For instance, Third Point Management and Trian Fund Management, holding only 2 percent of outstanding stock of Dow Chemical and Du Pont respectively, engineered a merger-and-split of America's top two chemical giants, as mentioned in Section 1.

Moreover, activist shareholders can easily circumvent the 5 percent rule by forming wolf packs. It is now a common practice for hedge funds to collaborate among themselves or with other institutional shareholders around a target company and coordinate their strategies and tactics. Even if each of those

---

[171] Refer to SEC's concerns when enacting Investment Act 1940, discussed in Section 2.
[172] Refer to Coffee and Palia (2016); Lu (2016); Brav et al. (2008); Briggs (2007).

collaborating holds less than 5 percent of the target company's outstanding shares, their combined stake can easily elevate them to the status of controlling shareholders. It is also possible for one lead wolf to take a share exceeding 5 percent, make public its intention of campaign, and then recruit other unidentified wolves, each holding less than 5 percent shares, to support the lead wolf's attack. In the fight over control of Barnes and Noble, for example, the lead activist held an 18.7 percent stake in the company, but it turned out that the actual wolf pack controlled a 36.14 percent stake.[173] In the campaign that forced the sale of Knight Ridder, "[w]hat started out as a 19% stake effectively grew to 37% in just 48 hours. The campaign succeeded almost instantly."[174]

Moreover, the easier formation of wolf packs, in turn, made it easier for hedge-fund activists to manipulate the market through the "wolf-pack effect". Upon the announcement or leaking of information about the formation of a wolf pack, the stock market generally reacts positively. For instance, an international study on the wolf-pack effect reports "abnormal announcement returns of 7% for the United States during a (-20, 20) day window" and of "6.4% and 4.8%, respectively", for Europe and Asia.[175] Those in the pack can easily develop trading strategies in advance because they exclusively know when they will trigger the wolf-pack effect. The market will also react to the way in which the wolves are moving together after the formation of the pack becomes public knowledge. Those in the pack again have advance knowledge of how they will act and can profit from front-running the market movements they create. The development of the derivatives market made it a lot easier for them to profit from front-running without being detected by regulators for market manipulation.

If both the anti-cartel spirit of the 5 percent rule and the anti-manipulation spirit are so easily compromised, the SEC should have tightened up the proxy rule to make it difficult for wolf packs to form and to profit from wolf pact effects. But the SEC has so far neither admitted the failure of the proxy rule change nor done anything to reverse the rule. This inaction only strengthens suspicion that the SEC, "self-regulating body", is in effect functioning as a promoter of financial interests captured by shareholder activists who simply clamor for more power and freedom for themselves.

Allowing free communication and engagement with management has similarly failed to bring about market-efficient outcomes mainly because shareholders do not have equal access to management. While corporate executives can ill afford not to be serious in communicating and engaging with big institutional shareholders, they can simply ignore or offer perfunctory replies

---

[173] Lu (2016, p. 778).   [174] Briggs (2007, pp. 682 698).
[175] Becht et al. (2017, pp. 29, 30, 34).

to the demands of small shareholders, who lack the larger players' resources. A critical question here is whether big institutional shareholders and other influential activists engage with management as impartial representatives of the general interests of shareholders or exploit their access to management mainly for their own gain. Common sense, as well as broad anecdotal evidence of institutions' self-serving utilization of communication and engagement with management, favors the latter answer.[176]

Calio and Zahralddin (1994) pointed out that free communication and engagement with management provides institutional shareholders with a "tactical edge over the management and small shareholders because it occurs behind-the-scenes without media scrutiny or individual investor awareness" (pp. 522–523). Cioffi (2006) similarly concluded:

> "The 1992 proxy rule changes appear to have encouraged greater governance by institutional shareholders, but at the expense of transparency. Institutional share-holders, with some notable exceptions, preferred to voice their concerns and criticisms to management in private communications that would not become public. These communications thus became occasions for managers to disclose significant information to the representatives of institutional shareholders and analysts associated with investment banks and brokerages" (p. 544).

In addition, the free communication rule, far from evening the aforementioned imbalance between shareholders and management, intensified the imbalance skewed to shareholders. Activist shareholders are now free to criticize the company's management "as long as the statements [they make] are not fraudulent."[177] In contentious issues, management makes its decisions by weighing their advantages and disadvantages. But activists can just focus on their perceived disadvantages and find whatever faults with management within the boundary of "not being fraudulent." It is even possible to criticize manage-ment for not achieving better performance in the name of maximizing share-holder value when the company concerned has been performing well. On the other hand, it is not often easy for management to criticize the company's activist shareholders unless it finds something seriously wrong with their statements or their behavior.

---

[176] For instance, some public pension fund administrators exploited the occasion of engagements for their own career development. Romano (1993, p. 822) relates that many public pension fund managers desire elective office and therefore enhance their political reputations by becoming crusaders against the interests of large corporations. "For instance, Elizabeth Holtzman, New York City comptroller and a trustee for the city's pension funds, publicized her active approach to corporate governance while campaigning for the Democratic party's nomination for U.S. Senator." Union pension funds are also found to use their engagement and proposals as "bargaining chips to provide the union with a private benefit" (Matsusaka et al. 2018, pp. 3222–3223).

[177] Calio and Zahralddin (1994, pp. 522–523).

Owing to the free-communication rule, it has now become a convention among hedge-fund activists to criticize management, not only by sending letters but also by publishing "white papers" and even convening press conferences. This kind of public criticism puts enormous pressure on management and, rather than considering the public warfare, company executives tend to prefer making compromises with activists by yielding to some of their demands. Daniel Loeb's (Third Point) attack on Dow Chemical is a case in point. Loeb opened a website specifically designed to criticize Dow management and their alleged "broken promises". Dow management gave in and accepted two directors nominated by Loeb in return for a one-year truce including the closure of the website. These two directors were under Loeb's "golden leashes" and soon played a central role in pushing Dow Chemical to conclude the merge-and-split deal with DuPont in December 2015.[178]

5.5 "Co-Investments" between Hedge-Fund Activists and Institutional Shareholders

Hedge-fund activists exert influence over corporations far beyond their shareholding because they often receive support from institutional shareholders implicitly or explicitly. The close ties between hedge-fund activists are multi-faceted. As financial investors, they share a similar world outlook that is focused on value extraction, which is different from corporate managers whose main responsibility is to create corporate value by producing high-quality, low-cost goods and services. Fund managers in institutional shareholders are also evaluated by their short-term performance even if they claim to pursue long-term gains. In this incentive structure, they tend to ally with hedge-fund activists. A Fortune report following the release of a letter to CEOs from BlackRock head Laurence Fink in 2014 that urged a long-term approach offers a vivid illustration:

> [T]aking a very small survey of companies in the S&P 500, [we] immediately ran into two that said the BlackRock analysts covering them had their own short-term demands–for good quarterly results. 'My guy's a fanatic,' reported the CEO of one of those companies. So it cannot be said that Fink's letter has even influenced the whole of BlackRock.[179]

---

[178] Refer to 'Dan Loeb Releases A Mini-Documentary Slamming Dow Chemical's Board For 'Broken Promises'' (www.businessinsider.com.au/dan-loeb-video-on-dow-chemical-2014-11); 'Loeb Unveils Website In New Era Of Dow Chemical Campaign' (www.valuewalk.com/2014/11/value-dow-dan-loeb/); 'Third Point Revives 'Golden Leash' Pay Plan in Dow Chemical Fight' (www.wsj.com/articles/third-point-revives-golden-leash-pay-plan-in-dow-chemical-fight-1416171616).

[179] Loomis (2014).

The 1996 NSMIA provided a strong impetus to convert the potential ties between hedge-fund activists and institutional shareholders into "co-investments," taking shares in the same company and coordinating their actions. Institutional shareholders already share commercial interests with hedge-fund activists because they supply about 60 percent of hedge funds' AUM. Institutional shareholders apparently maintain the practice of voting independently of hedge-fund activists, which is legally required of them. However, if an institutional shareholder holds shares in both the hedge fund and the targeted company, it is highly likely to side with the hedge fund to raise the overall yield of its holding in the company and its alternative investment in the hedge fund. Anecdotal evidence of co-investment abounds.

For instance, it was revealed during the proxy battle between DuPont and Trian Partners that the California Teachers Retirement System (CaLSTRS) had cooperated with Trian's campaign from the beginning. According to a Fortune report, DuPont's management had never thought of this possibility because CalSTRS was a long-term shareholder and the company "generally had a congenial working relationship with the pension fund". But CalSTRS co-signed an early letter supporting Trian when the latter attacked DuPont in 2015 and turned out later to be one of the hedge fund's major investors. In detailing how DuPont went to war with Trian, the report stated that "[t]ies like that have made it harder for companies like DuPont to argue that siding with activists isn't in the interest of shareholders."[180]

The most detailed account of co-investment revealed in public so far has probably been that between CalSTRS and Relational Investors, an activist hedge fund set up by Ralph V. Whitworth and David H. Batchelder, who used to work with T. Boone Pickens as fellow corporate raiders.[181] CalSTRS committed $1 billion to Relational, $300 million to Trian, and $100 million to Starboard in 2013. Working in tandem from the beginning, Relational and CalSTRS increased their participation in Timken, a fifth-generation family business producing high-quality steel and bearings, until the holding of each reached the 5% threshold for a 13D filing. As part of their attempt to push the Timken family into breaking the company into two separate entities and increasing stock buybacks, Relational and CalSTRS set up a website, "unlock-timken.com", that criticized Timken management publicly. An investment officer from CalSTRS joined a roadshow organized by Relational, flying to New York to meet fellow pension-fund managers. A seat on the Timken board was filled by a CalSTRS representative, and "the pension fund, long a champion of better corporate governance, made the case that Timken's board was

---

[180] Gandel (2015).   [181] The details are from Schwartz (2014); Orol (2014); Denning (2014).

dominated by family members who paid themselves liberally and put their own interests ahead of shareholders' interests."[182] In April 2012, three weeks before the proxy vote, Relational and CalSTRS put out a news release calling Tim Timken's $9 million pay package in 2011 "grossly out-of-line with other executive chairmen in Timken's peer group."[183] Their proposal to split the company into Timken and TimkenSteel eventually garnered 53 percent of shareholder votes.

6 Conclusions: Rebuilding the Proxy Voting and Engagement System

In this Element, I have emphasized the detachment of the rhetoric of shareholder democracy from its reality, or the disconnection between value creation and value extraction, in the evolution of shareholder activism. Predatory value extraction by hedge-fund activists is a result of regulatory changes in the 1980s and 1990s that strengthened the value extracting power of shareholder activists without understanding their effects on the value creation process. This confusion between value creation and extraction is evident in SEC's Final Rule on compulsory voting of mutual funds in 2003, where it referred to the new rule's effects on "capital formation" as follows:

> The rule and rule amendments will likely increase investor confidence in investment advisers by making proxy voting more transparent and encouraging increased emphasis on proxy voting by advisers. Because capital formation is influenced by investor confidence in the markets, we believe that the rule could have a positive effect on capital markets.[184]

"Investor confidence," essentially institutional shareholders' confidence in value extraction, is treated here as a panacea as if it will solve everything, including "capital formation," which is value creation at the economy level. The three pillars of the SEC's mission are (1) to protect investors, (2) to maintain fair, orderly, and efficient markets, and (3) to facilitate capital formation.[185] The statement quoted above is no more than proof that the SEC does not have an idea about how to facilitate capital formation in the economy and uses its mission of capital formation only rhetorically.

---

[182] Schwartz (2014).

[183] Relational Investors and CalSTRS press release, "Relational Investors LLC and CalSTRS Urge Timken's Board to Take Action to Separate the Company's Businesses to Unlock Shareholder Value," February 19, 2013, www.businesswire.com/news/home/20130219006721/en/Relational-Investors-LLC-CalSTRS-Urge-Timken%E2%80%99s-Board.

[184] Securities and Exchange Commission (2003), 'Final Rule: Proxy Voting by Investment Advisers,' *U.S. Securities and Exchange Commission*, www.sec.gov/rules/final/ia-2106.htm.

[185] The SEC website, www.sec.gov/about/mission (Accessed on January 28, 2024).

This Element showed that the current proxy voting and engagement system undermines all three pillars. First, the current system protects only the strong and active shareholders instead of protecting public shareholders in general. "Free communication and engagement" are effectively available to hedge-fund activists and corporate governance teams in large institutional shareholders. Second, the "wolf-pack effect" manifests that the system allows unfair, unruly, and manipulated markets instead of fair, orderly, and efficient ones. Third, as discussed in Section 4, it facilitates value extraction, even to the extent of predatory value extraction, instead of capital formation. If regulatory changes have failed to bring about their intended effects, they should be reversed or recalibrated. Therefore, I propose the following recommendations to rebuild the proxy voting and engagement system to support sustainable value creation and extraction.

First, the SEC should make it mandatory for the shareholders to submit justifications in their proposals on corporate value creation or capital formation. When activist shareholders propose to disgorge free cash flows by increasing stock buybacks or dividends, they argue that a certain amount of cash flow is "free," meaning that it does not affect the corporation's operations. But they never explain why the "disgorging" is good or at least neutral for value creation and corporate sustainability. By requiring justifications for value creation in their proposals, shareholders can discuss these reasons openly before voting.

This new regulation will also force corporate executives to think and behave in line with balancing value creation and extraction. If it is mandatory for public shareholders to provide justifications for value creation, corporate executives should adequately prepare responses to those claims. Corporate executives will thereby devote their efforts more to balancing value creation and extraction. The new regulation would then transform the proxy voting system into an arena where shareholders and management can discuss practical ways to promote sustainable value creation and extraction.

Second, voting should be removed as a fiduciary duty of institutional shareholders. The compulsory and open voting by uninterested and incapable institutional shareholders gave illegitimate power to proxy advisory firms and allowed hedge-fund activists to exploit the vacuum in proxy voting. The SEC should acknowledge the unintended consequences of compulsory voting and how institutional activism has deviated from the ideal behavior in proxy voting. Institutional shareholders can then decide to vote, as with political voting. As a result, only those keen on contributing to sustainable value creation and extraction would join the proxy voting arena.

Third, the SEC should encourage differentiated voting rights favoring long-term shareholders. Value creation takes time to overcome uncertainties through strategic control, organizational integration, and financial commitment. It is, therefore, natural that long-term shareholders are more supportive of value creation than short-term shareholders. However, the prevailing financial regulations do not distinguish between the long-term and the short-term shareholders, even when policy-makers and senior SEC officials voice their concerns about "short-termism."

Many European countries practice differentiated voting rights systems for shares controlled by management and those held by public shareholders. For instance, France adopted the Florange Act in 2014, whereby shares registered for two years automatically receive double voting rights. Similarly, Italy introduced the mechanism of loyalty shares, allowing listed companies to grant up to a maximum of two votes per share to those shareholders who have continuously held their shares for at least two years. Netherlands and Nordic countries have long exercised differentiated voting rights. In Europe, the principal purpose of the differentiated voting rights system according to holding period is to encourage longer-term holding and discourage short-termism.[186]

In the United States, it is relatively easy to issue dual-class shares before a company is publicly listed, but it is difficult to issue dual-class shares after a public listing. Institutional shareholders, led by the Council of Institutional Shareholders (CII), have long advocated abolishing the dual-class share system because they consider the system simply as a tool to protect the entrenched founders and the management.[187] However, institutional shareholders are diverse in their objectives and method of holding shares. According to a McKinsey study, short-term investors hold only 25 percent of US stocks, while long-term investors hold 75 percent.[188] If multiple voting rights are given proportionate to the holding periods, like in the Netherlands and Nordic countries, many institutional shareholders would support this new regulation. One can then envisage establishing a "holy alliance" between longer-term institutional shareholders and value-creating executives, replacing the current "unholy alliance" between activist shareholders and value-extracting executives. Furthermore, this new system encouraging long-term shareholding would be

---

[186] For Europe's various differentiated voting systems, refer to Ventoruzzo (2015); Shearman & Sterling (2016); Stothard (2015); Shin (2015); 'Differentiated Voting Rights in Europe,' The ISS website, www.issgovernance.com/analysis-differentiated-voting-rights-in-europe/ (last visited on July 19, 2021).

[187] It states as follows, ""One share, one vote" is a bedrock principle of good corporate governance. When a company taps the capital markets to raise money from public investors, those investors should have a right to vote in proportion to the size of their holdings. A single class of common stock with equal voting rights also ensures that the board of directors is accountable to all of the shareholders." 'Dual-Class Stock', CII website, http://www.cii.org/dualclass_stock (accessed on January 30, 2024).

[188] Darr and Koller (2017).

consistent with the interests of institutional shareholders' ultimate customers – pensioners and ordinary savers.

Fourth, the SEC should make it mandatory for shareholders and management to publicly disclose their engagement session discussions. Currently, "free engagement" is only available to some influential investors. Powerful investors prefer "private communication," which makes the engagement sessions become occasions for managers to disclose significant information.[189] Fund managers whose compensation packages are critically dependent on their trading performance have every incentive to exploit undisclosed information for trading. But even if corporate managers recognize that those fund managers are utilizing insider information acquired from engagement sessions, they cannot report it to the regulatory authorities because they would be penalized for revealing it to fund managers. The SEC has sought to prohibit "fraud and deceit," including profiting from insider information, and there is no reason why an engagement should be an exception.

Fifth, hedge funds should be regulated commensurate with institutional shareholders. Hedge funds are powerful enough to pose systemic risks to the economy, as we witnessed with the collapse of Long-Term Capital Management (LTCM) in 1998 and the subsequent government-led rescue to protect the financial system from collapse.[190] Since the passing of the 1996 NSMIA, hedge funds have managed a large portion of institutional shareholders' funds to benefit ordinary workers and pensioners. There is no reason why hedge funds should remain treated as "private entities" and not subject to financial regulations applied to institutional shareholders because hedge funds effectively function as institutional shareholders. Dayen (2016) points out, "[t]heir emergence was an accident of history, a gift to wealthy families. But the by-product of that gift has now grown to outsized proportions and shoved itself into practically every aspect of economic life." The SEC should put hedge funds under the Investment Act of 1940, mandate disclosure of their shareholdings, and regulate their use of leverage accordingly.

Sixth, the SEC should raise barriers against wolf packs and co-investment to strengthen its policing of collusive behaviors among investors. The 1992 proxy rule amendments allowed *de facto* investor cartels. Any policy encouraging investor cartels cannot be justified under the SEC's mission. The SEC should significantly lower the 5 percent threshold where investor cartels cannot work. It should also make it mandatory for hedge funds to publicly disclose the institutional shareholders who provide their AUM and hold shares of the companies they campaign against.

---

[189] Cioffi (2006). Quoted in Section 5.4.

[190] Lowenstein (2002); Edwards (1999); Department of the Treasury, Board of Governors of the Federal Reserve System, Securities and Exchange Commission, Commodity Futures Trading Commission (1999).

References

Ahuja, Maneet (2012), *The Alpha Masters*, John Wiley.

Ayres, Robert and Michael Olenick (2017), "Secular Stagnation (or Corporate Suicide?)," *Insead Working Paper*, https://ruayres.wordpress.com/2017/07/11/secular-stagnation-or-corporate-suicide/.

Bainbridge, Stephen M. (2005), "Shareholder Activism and Institutional Investors," *UCLA School of Law, Law-Econ Research Paper* 05–20, https://papers.ssrn.com/sol3/papers.cfm?abstract_id=796227.

Bebchuk, Lucian and Scott Hirst (2019), "Index Funds and the Future of Corporate Governance: Theory, Evidence, and Policy," *Columbia Law Review* 119(8): 2029–2146.

Bebchuk, Lucian, Alon Brav and Wei Jiang (2015), "The Long-Term Effects of Hedge-Fund Activism," *Columbia Law Review* 115(5): 1085–1155.

Becht, Marco, Julian Franks, Jeremy Grant and Hammes F. Wagner (2017), "Returns to Hedge Fund Activism: An International Study," *The Review of Financial Studies* 30(9): 2933–2971.

Berle, Adolf A. and Gardiner C. Means (1932), *Modern Corporation and Private Property*, MacMillan.

Bethel, Jennifer E. and Stuart L. Gillan (2002), "The Impact of the Institutional and Regulatory Environment on Shareholder Voting," *Financial Management* 31(4): 29–54.

Bew, Robyn and Richard Fields (2012), "Voting Decisions at US Mutual Funds: How Investors Really Use Proxy Advisers," https://ssrn.com/abstract=2084231.

Bhagat, Sanjai, Bernard Black and Margaret Blair (2004), "Relational Investing and Firm Performance," *Journal of Financial Research* 27(1): 1–30.

Biggs, John H. (2005), *Keynote Speech, Institutional Investors as Owners Conference at the Stern School of Business*, New York University (NYU).

Birch, Sarah (2009), *Full Participation: A Comparative Study of Compulsory Voting*, Manchester University Press.

Blair, Margaret (1995), *Ownership and Control: Rethinking Corporate Governance for the Twenty-First Century*, The Brookings Institution.

Blair, Margaret (2003a), *Corporate Governance and Capital Flows in a Global Economy*, Oxford University Press.

Blair, Margaret (2003b), "Locking in Capital: What Corporate Law Achieved for Business Organizers in the Nineteenth Century," *UCLA Law Review* 51(2): 387–455.

Bogle, John (2005), *The Battle for the Soul of Capitalism*, Yale University Press.

Boyarsky, Bill (2007), *Big Daddy: Jesse Unruh and the Art of Power Politics*, University of California Press.

Brav, Alon, John R. Graham, Campbell R. Harvey and Roni Michaely (2005), "Payout Policy in the 21st Century," *Journal of Financial Economics* 77(3): 483–527.

Brav, Alon, Wei Jiang and Hyunseob Kim (2010), "Hedge Fund Activism: Review," *Foundations and Trends in Finance* 4(3): 1–66.

Brav, Alon, Wei Jiang, Frank Partnoy and Randall Frank Thomas (2008), "Hedge Fund Activism, Corporate Governance and Firm Performance," *Journal of Finance* 63(4): 1729–1775.

Brennan, Jason and Lisa Hill (2014), *Compulsory Voting: For and against*, Cambridge University Press.

Brav, A., Jiang, W., & Kim, H. (2015). The Real Effects of Hedge Fund Activism: Productivity, Asset Allocation, and Labor Outcomes. *Review of Financial Studies*, 28(10).

Briggs, Thomas W. (2007), "Corporate Governance and the New Hedge Fund Activism: An Empirical Analysis," *Journal of Corporation Law* 32(4): 682–738.

Burger, Dani (2017), "The U.S. Stock Market Belongs to Bots," *Bloomberg*, www.bloomberg.com/news/articles/2017-06-15/it-s-a-quant-s-stock-mar ket-as-computer-programs-keep-on-buying.

Calio, Joseph Evan and Rafael Xavier Zahralddin (1994), "The Securities and Exchange Commission's 1992 Proxy Amendments: Questions of Accountability," *Pace Law Review* 14(2): 460–539.

Chandler, Alfred (1962), *Strategy and Structure: Chapters in the History of the American Industrial Enterprise*, MIT Press.

Chandler, Alfred (1977), *The Visible Hand: The Managerial Revolution in American Business*, Harvard University Press.

Chandler, Alfred (1990). *Scale and Scope*, Harvard University Press.

Chandler, Beverly (2016), "Event Driven Paper Finds Investors Disenchanted," *AlphaQ*, www.alphaq.world/2016/06/20/240734/event-driven-paper-finds-investors-disenchanted.

Cheffins, Brian R. (2013), "The History of Corporate Governance," in Mike Wright, Donald S. Siegel, Kevin Keasey, and Igor Filatotchev (2013) (eds.), *The Oxford Handbook of Corporate Governance* 54. https://doi.org/10.1093/oxfordhb/9780199642007.001.0001.

Cheffins, Brian R. and John Armour (2011), "The Past, Present, and Future of Shareholder Activism by Hedge Funds," *The Journal of Corporation Law* 37(1): 51–103.

Cheng, Yingmei, Jarrad Harford and Tianming Zhang (2015), "Bonus-Driven Repurchases," *Journal of Financial and Quantitative Analysis* 50(3): 447–475.

Cioffi, John W. (2006), "Corporate Governance Reform, Regulatory Politics, and the Foundations of Finance Capitalism in the United States and Germany," *German Law Journal* 7(6): 533–561.

Coates IV, John C. (2018), "The Future of Corporate Governance Part I: The Problem of Twelve," *Harvard Public Law Working Paper 19–07.*

Coffee, John C. (2012), "Dispersed Ownership: The Theories, the Evidence, and the Enduring Tension between 'Lumpers' and 'Splitters'," in Mueller, Dennis C. (ed.), *The Oxford Handbook of Capitalism*, Oxford University Press.

Coffee, John C. and Darius Palia (2016), "The Wolf at the Door: The Impact of Hedge Fund Activism on Corporate Governance," *Annals of Corporate Governance* 1(1): 1–94.

Council of Institutional Investors (2024), "Dual-Class Stock," *Council of Institutional Investors*, www.cii.org/dualclass_stock.

Craig, Sussane (2013), "The Giant of Shareholders, Quietly Stirring," *The New York Times*, www.nytimes.com/2013/05/19/business/blackrock-a-share holding-giant-is-quietly-stirring.html.

Crowther, Samuel (1929), "Everybody Ought to Be Rich: An Interview with John J. Raskob" *Ladies' Home Journal.* https://wp.lps.org/kbeacom/files/ 2012/08/EverybodyOughtToBeRich.pdf.

Danneman, Justin (2017), "A.I. Controls the Stock Market," *Squawker*, https:// squawker.org/analysis/robots-control-the-stock-markets/.

Darr, Rebecca and Tim Koller (2017), "How to Build an Alliance against Corporate Short-termism, McKinsey & Company," www.mckinsey.com/busi ness-functions/strategy-and-corporate-finance/our-insights/how-to-build-an-alliance-against-corporate-short-termism. (last visited February 7, 2021).

Dayen, David (2016), "What Good Are Hedge Funds?" *The American Prospect*, http://prospect.org/article/what-good-are-hedge-funds.

deHaan, David Larcker and Charles McClure (2019), "Long-Term Economic Consequences of Hedge Fund Activist Interventions," *Review of Accounting Studies* 24(2): 536–569.

Demsetz, Harold (1995), *The Economics of the Business Firm: Seven Critical Commentaries.* Cambridge University Press.

Denes, Matthew R., Jonathan M. Karpoff and Victoria B. McWilliams (2017), "Thirty Years of Shareholder Activism: A Survey of Empirical Research," *Journal of Corporate Finance* 44: 405–424.

Denning, Steve (2014), "When Pension Funds Become Vampires," *Forbes*, www .forbes.com/sites/stevedenning/2014/12/10/when-pension-funds-become-vampires/#704aac67510c.

Department of the Treasury, Board of Governors of the Federal Reserve System, Securities and Exchange Commission, Commodity Futures Trading Commission (1999), "Hedge Funds, Leverage, and the Lessons of Long-Term Capital Management," *Report of the President's Working Group on Financial Markets*, www.cftc.gov/sites/default/files/tm/tmhedgefundreport.htm.

Dodd-Frank Act (2011), "Section 404, 'Final Rule'," www.sec.gov/rules/final/2011/ia-3308.pdf.

Drucker, Peter (1976), *The Unseen Revolution: How Pension Fund Socialism Came to America*, Harper & Row.

Edwards, Franklin R. (1999), "Hedge Funds and the Collapse of Long-Term Capital Management," *Journal of Economic Perspectives* 13(2): 189–210.

Fama, Eugene F. (1980), "Agency Problems and the Theory of the Firm," *Journal of Political Economy* 88(2).

Fama, Eugene F. and Michael Jensen (1983), "Separation of Ownership and Control," *Journal of Law & Economics* 26(2).

Foley, Steven (2016), "The So-Called Death of Event-Driven Investing," *Financial Times*, www.ft.com/content/cc45d8ee-e135-11e5-9217-6ae3733a2cd1.

Foley, Steven and Miles Johnson (2014), "'Event-Driven' Hedge Funds Leap into Lead after Rush to Invest," Financial Times, www.ft.com/content/d9a8b122-d61b-11e3-a239-00144feabdc0.

Gandel, Stephen (2015), "How DuPont Went to War with Activist Investor Nelson Peltz," *Fortune*, http://fortune.com/2015/05/11/how-dupont-went-to-war/.

Gelter, Martin (2013), "The Pension System and the Rise of Shareholder Primacy," *Seton Hall Law Review* 43(3): 909–970.

Gillan, Stuart and Laura T. Starks (2007), "The Evolution of Shareholder Activism in the United States," *Journal of Applied Corporate Finance* 19(1): 55–73.

Glass Lewis (2024), "Company Overview," *Glass Lewis*, www.glasslewis.com/company-overview/.

Hansmann, Henry and Reinier Kraakman (2000), "The Essential Role of Organizational Law." *Yale Law Journal* 110.

Hopkins, Matt and William Lazonick (2016), "The Mismeasure of Mammon: The Uses and Abuses of Executive Pay Data," *Institute for New Economic Thinking Working Paper No. 49*, www.ineteconomics.org/research/research-papers/the-mismeasure-of-mammon-uses-and-abuses-of-executive-pay-data.

Iliev, Peter and Michelle Lowry (2015), "Are Mutual Funds Active Voters?" *Review of Financial Studies* 28(2): 446–485.

Investment Company Act of 1940 (1940), www.govinfo.gov/content/pkg/COMPS-1879/pdf/COMPS-1879.pdf.

ISS (2017), "Analysis: Differentiated Voting Rights in Europe," *ISS*, www .issgovernance.com/analysis-differentiated-voting-rights-in-europe/.

ISS (2024), "About ISS," *ISS*, www.issgovernance.com/about/about-iss/.

Jensen, Michael (1986), "Agency Costs of Free Cash Flow, Corporate Finance, and Takeovers," *American Economic Review* 76(2): 323–329.

Jensen, Michael (1988), "Takeovers: The Causes and Consequences," *Journal of Economic Perspective* 2(1).

Jensen, Michael (1989), "Eclipse of the Public Corporation," *Harvard Business Review* 67(5): 61–74.

Jensen, Michael (1993), "The Modern Industrial Revolution, Exit, and the Failure of Internal Control Systems," *Journal of Finance* 48(3): 831–880.

Jensen, Michael and Kevin Murphy (1990), "Performance Pay and Top Management Incentives," *Journal of Political Economy* 98(2): 225–264.

Jensen, Michael and William H. Meckling (1976), "Theory of the Firm: Managerial Behavior, Agency Costs and Ownership Structure," *Journal of Financial Economics* 3(4): 305–360.

Karpoff, Jonathan M. (2001), "The Impact of Shareholder Activism on Target Companies: A Survey of Empirical Findings," *SSRN Electronic Journal*, https://doi.org/10.2139/ssrn.885365.

Kolhatkar, Sheelah (2018), "Paul Singer, Doomsday Investor," *New Yorker*, www.newyorker.com/magazine/2018/08/27/paul-singer-doomsday-investor.

Kumar, Nikhil (2012), "The Vulture Capitalist Who Devoured Peru – And Now Threatens Argentina," *The Independent*, www.independent.co.uk/news/ world/americas/the-vulture-capitalist-who-devoured-peru-and-now-threatens-argentina-8347577.html.

Klein, William A. and John C. Coffee (2004) (9th ed.). *Business Organization and Finance: Legal and Economic Principles*. Thomson Reuters/Foundation Press

Laide, John (2014), "Activists Increasing Success Gaining Board Seats at U.S. Companies," *Shark Repellent*, www.sharkrepellent. net/request?an=dt .getPage&st= undefined&pg=/pub/rs_20140310. html&rnd=176396.

Laster, Travis J. and John Mark Zeberkiewicz, (2014), "The Rights and Duties of Blockholder Directors," *The Business Lawyer* 70(1): 33–60.

Lazonick, William (1991), *Business Organization and the Myth of the Market Economy*, Cambridge University Press.

Lazonick, William (1992), "Controlling the Market for Corporate Control." *Industrial and Corporate Change* 1(3).

Lazonick, William (2007), "The U.S. Stock Market and the Governance of Innovative Enterprise," *Industrial and Corporate Change* 16(6): 1021–1022.

Lazonick, William (2013), "The Financialization of the US Corporation: What Has Been Lost, and How It Can Be Regained," *Seattle University Law Review* 36(2): 857–909.

Lazonick, William (2014a), "Innovative Enterprise and Shareholder Value," *Law and Financial Markets Review* 8(1): 52–64.

Lazonick, William (2014b), "Profits without Prosperity: Stock Buybacks Manipulate the Market and Leave Most Americans Worse Off," *Harvard Business Review*, September: 46–55.

Lazonick, William (2015), "The Theory of Innovative Enterprise: Foundation of Economic Analysis," *Academic-Industry Research Working Paper* #13–0201.

Lazonick, William (2019), "The Value-Extracting CEO: How Executive Stock-Based Pay Undermines Investment in Productive Capabilities," *Structural Change and Economic Dynamics* 60.

Lazonick, William (2022), "Is the Most Unproductive Firm the Foundation of the Most Efficient Economy? Penrosian Learning and the Neoclassical Fallacy," *International Review of Applied Economics*, 36(2): 1–32. And Lazonick "Corporate Governance for the Common Good."

Lazonick, William (2023), *Investing in Innovation: Confronting Predatory Value Extraction in the US Corporation*, Cambridge University Press.

Lazonick, William and Jang-Sup Shin (2020), *Predatory Value Extraction: How the Looting of the Business Enterprise Became the US Norm and How Sustainable Prosperity Can Be Restored*, Oxford University Press.

Lazonick, William and Ken Jacobson (2022), "Letter to SEC: How Stock Buybacks Undermine Investment in Innovation for the Sake of Stock-Price Manipulation," Institute for New Economic Thinking, www.ineteconomics .org/perspectives/blog/letter-to-sec-a-policy-framework-for-attaining-sus tainable-prosperity-in-the-united-states.

Lazonick, William and Mary O'Sullivan (1997), "Finance and Industrial Development, Part I: The United States and the United Kingdom," *Financial History Review* 4(1): 7–29.

Lazonick, William and Mary O'Sullivan (2000), "American Corporate Finance," in Howes, Candace and Ajit Singh (eds.), *Competitiveness Matters*, Michigan University Press.

Lazonick, William, Matt Hopkins and Ken Jacobson (2016), "What We Learn about Inequality from Carl Icahn's $2 Billion Apple 'No Brainer'," Institute for New Economic Thinking, www.ineteconomics.org/perspectives/blog/what-we-learn-about-inequality-from-carl-icahns-2-billion-apple-no-brainer.

Lever, Annabelle (2010), "Compulsory Voting: A Critical Perspective," *British Journal of Political Science* 40(4): 897–915.

Loomis, Carol (1966), "The Jones Nobody Keeps Up with," *Fortune*, http://fortune.com/2015/12/29/hedge-funds-fortune-1966/.

Loomis, Carol (1970), "Hard Times Come to the Hedge Funds," *Fortune*, http://archive.fortune.com/magazines/fortune/fortune_archive/1970/01/00/hedge_fund/pdf.html.

Loomis, Carol (2014), "BlackRock: The $4.3 Trillion Force," *Fortune*, http://fortune.com/2014/07/07/blackrock-larry-fink/.

Lowenstein, Roger (2002), *When Genius Failed: The Rise and Fall of Long-Term Capital Management*, Random House.

Lu, Carmen X. W., (2016), "Unpacking Wolf Packs," *Yale Law Journal* 125(3).

Lund, Dorothy S. (2018), "The Case against Passive Shareholder Voting," *Journal of Corporation Law* 43(3).

Machan, Dyan and Riva Atlas (1994), "George Soros, Meet A.W. Jones," *Forbes*, p. 43.

Malanga, Steven (2013), "The Pension Fund That Ate California," *City Journal*, www.city-journal.org/html/pension-fund-ate-california-13528.html.

Manconi, Alberto, Urs Peyer and Theo Vermaelen (2018), "Are Buybacks Good for Long-Term Shareholder Value? Evidence from Buybacks around the World," *Journal of Financial and Quantitative Analysis* 54(5): 1–74.

Marriage, Madison (2013), "Activist Investors Fuel Event-Driven Returns," *Financial Times*, www.ft.com/content/faafbd08-ea1b-11e2-b2f4-00144feabdc0.

Matsusaka, John G., Oguzhan Ozbas, Irene Yi (2018), "'Opportunistic Proposals by Union Shareholders," USC CLASS Research Paper No. CLASS15-25, Marshall School of Business Working Paper No. 17-3, https://ssrn.com/abstract=2666064 or http://dx.doi.org/10.2139/ssrn.2666064.

McGrattan, Ellen R. and Edward C. Prescott (2004), "The 1929 Stock Market: Irving Fischer Was Right," *International Economic Review* 45(4).

Merced, Michael (2016), "Samsung in Cross Hairs of American Hedge Fund," *New York Times*, http://nyti.ms/2dxarIk.

Merle, Renae (2016), "How One Hedge Fund Made $2 Billion from Argentina's Economic Collapse," *Washington Post*, www.washingtonpost.com/news/business/wp/2016/03/29/how-one-hedge-fund-made-2-billion-from-argentinas-economic-collapse/?utm_term=.ac20762574d7.

Meyer, Gregory, Nicole Bullock and Joe Rennison (2018), "How High-Frequency Trading Hit a Speed Bump," Financial Times, January 1, 2018, www.ft.com/content/d81f96ea-d43c-11e7-a303-9060cb1e5f44.

Mirae Asset (2017), "The Current State and Direction of Samsung Electronics' Stock Buybacks," Mirae Asset Daily Report, September 15 (in Korean).

Monks, Robert (2013), "Robert Monks: It's Broke, Let's Fix It," *Listed Magazine*, http://listedmag.com/2013/06/robert-monks-its-broke-lets-fix-it.

Monks, Robert (2015), "Careless Language or Cunning Propaganda," *RFK Compass event*, www.ragm.com/libraryFiles/145.pdf.

Nathan, Charles (2010), *The Parallel Universes of Institutional Investing and Institutional Voting*, Institutional Investors.

Orol, Ronald (2014), "Teaming up with CalSTRS Helps Activist Funds Get Their Way," *Harvard Roundtable on Shareholder Engagement – Consolidated Background Materials*, www.law.harvard.edu/programs/corp_gov/share holder-engagement-roundtable-2015-materials/Harvard-Roundtable-on-Shareholder-Engagement-Consolidated-Background-Materials.pdf.

Ott, Julia C. (2011), *When Wall Street Met Main Street: The Quest for Investors' Democracy*, Harvard University Press.

Parisian, Elizabeth and Saqib Bhatti (2016), "All That Glitters Is Not Gold – An Analysis of US Public Pension Investments in Hedge Funds," Roosevelt Institute, http://rooseveltinstitute.org/wp-content/uploads/2015/12/All-That-Glitters-Is-Not-Gold-Nov-2015.pdf.

Perino, Michael (2010), *The Hellhound of Wall Street: How Ferdinand Pecora's Investigation of the Great Crash Forever Changed American Finance*, Penguin Press.

Pichhadze, Aviv (2010), "Private Equity, Ownership, and Regulation," *The Journal of Private Equity* 14(1): 17–24.

Pichhadze, Aviv (2012), "Institutional Investors as Blockholders," in Vasudev, P.M. and Susan Watson (eds.), *Corporate Governance after the Financial Crisis*, Edgar Elgar.

Preqin (2016), "2016 Preqin Global Hedge Fund Report – Sample pages," www.preqin.com/docs/samples/2016-Preqin-Global-Hedge-Fund-Report-Sample-Pages.pdf.

Reiff, Nathan (2017), "The Greatest Inventors," *Investopedia*, www.investope dia.com/university/greatest/.

Robé, Jean-Philippe (2011), "The Legal Structure of the Firm," *Accounting, Economics, and Law: A Convivium* 1(1).

Roe, Mark J. (1990), "Political and Legal Restraints on Ownership and Control of Public Companies," *Journal of Financial Economics* 27(1).

Roe, Mark J. (1991), "Political Elements in the Creation of Mutual Fund Industry," *University of Pennsylvania Law Review* 139(6).

Romano, Roberta (1993), "Public Pension Fund Activism in Corporate Governance Reconsidered," *Columbia Law Review* 93(4): 793–853.

Rose, Paul (2007), "The Corporate Governance Industry," *The Journal of Corporation Law* 32(4): 887–926.

Rosenberg, Hilary (1999), *A Traitor to His Class*, John Wiley.

Salmon, Felix and Jon Stokes (2010), "Algorithms Take Control of Wall Street," *Wired*, (www.wired.com/2010/12/ff_ai_flashtrading/?mbid=email_onsiteshare).

Schwartz, Nelson D. (2014), "How Wall Street Bent Steel: Timken Bows to Activist Investors, and Splits in Two," *The New York Times*, www.nytimes.com/2014/12/07/business/timken-bows-to-investors-and-splits-in-two.html?_r=0.

Securities and Exchange Commission (1969), "35th Annual Report," www.sec.gov/about/annual_report/1969.pdf.

Securities and Exchange Commission (1992), "Final Proxy Rule Amendments, Exchange Act," *Federal Securities Law Reporter* 34–31326.

Securities and Exchange Commission (2000), "Final Rule: Selective Disclosure and Insider Trading," *U.S. Securities and Exchange Commission*, www.sec.gov/rules/final/33-7881.htm.

Securities and Exchange Commission (2003), "Final Rule: Proxy Voting by Investment Advisers," *U.S. Securities and Exchange Commission*, www.sec.gov/rules/final/ia-2106.htm.

Securities and Exchange Commission (2017), "Private Funds Statistics – Second Calendar Quarter 2016," *U.S. Securities and Exchange Commission*, www.sec.gov/divisions/investment/private-funds-statistics/private-funds-statistics-2016-q2-accessible.pdf.

Securities Exchange Act of 1933 (1933), www.govinfo.gov/content/pkg/COMPS-1884/pdf/COMPS-1884.pdf.

Securities Exchange Act of 1934 (1934), www.govinfo.gov/content/pkg/COMPS-1885.pdf.

Sharara, Norma M. and Anne E. Hoke-Witherspoon (1993), "The Evolution of the 1992 Shareholder Communication Proxy Rules and Their Impact on Corporate Governance," *The Business Lawyer* 49(1): 327–358.

Shearman and Sterling (2016), "The Proportionality Principle in the European Union," *Report commissioned by the European Commission*, http://ec.europa.eu/internal_market/company/docs/shareholders/study/final_report_en.pdf.

Shin, Jang-Sup (2015), "The Reality of 'Actions' by Activist Hedge Funds and Public Policies on *Chaebols*," *The KERI Insight*, http://fiid.org/wp-content/uploads/2015/07/Activist-fund-and-chaebol-policy-KERI-Insight-2015-7-1.pdf.

Shu, Chong (2021), The Proxy Advisory Industry: Influencing and Being Influenced. Unpublished paper. www-scf.usc.edu/~chongshu/papers/shu2020proxy.pdf.

Shu, Chong (2024), "The Proxy Advisory Industry: Influencing and Being Influenced," *USC Marshall School of Business Research Paper*, http://dx.doi.org/10.2139/ssrn.3614314.

Singh, Shane P. (2015), "Compulsory Voting and the Turnout Decision Calculus," *Political Studies* 63(3): 548–568.

Smith, Michael P. (1996), "Shareholder Activism by Institutional Investors: Evidence from CalPERS," *The Journal of Finance* 51(1): 227–252.

Solomon, Steven Davidoff (2015), "Remaking Dow and DuPont for the Activist Shareholders," *The New York Times*, www.nytimes.com/2015/12/16/business/dealbook/remaking-dow-and-dupont-for-the-activist-shareholders.html?_r=0.

Stothard, Michael (2015), "French companies fight back against Florange double-vote law," *The Financial Times*, www.ft.com/content/05314dfe-e27d-11e4-ba33-00144feab7de.

Stout, Lynn (2013), "The Troubling Question of Corporate Purpose," Symposium on 'Shareholder Value Myth,' *Accounting, Economics, and Law: Convivium* 3(1), www.degruyter.com/view/j/ael.2013.3.issue-1/ael-2013-0042/ael-2013-0042.xml?f=&print&print.

Strickland, Deon, Kenneth Wiles and Marc Zenner (1996), "A Requiem for the USA – Is Small Shareholder Monitoring Effective?" *Journal of Financial Economics* 40(2): 319–338.

Strine, Jr Leo E. (2005), "The Delaware Way: How We Do Corporate Law and Some of the New Challenges We (and Europe) Face," *Delaware Journal of Corporate Law* 30(3): 673–696.

Strine, Jr Leo E. (2007), "Toward Common Sense and Common Ground? – Reflections on the Shared Interests of Managers and Labor in a More Rational System of Corporate Governance," *Harvard Law and Economics* Discussion Paper No. 585.

Stulz, René M. (2007), "Hedge Funds: Past, Present, and Future," *The Journal of Economic Perspectives* 21(2): 175–194.

Team, Tefis (2016), "Dissecting the Dow and DuPont deal, from Merger to Split?," *Forbes*, www.forbes.com/sites/greatspeculations/2016/08/30/dissecting-dow-and-dupont-deal-from-merger-to-split/#1414e3286967.

Traeger, Rebecca (2018), "DowDuPont Names Its Three New Separate Businesses," *Chemistry World*, www.chemistryworld.com/news/dowdupont-names-its-three-new-separate-businesses/3008721.article.

U.S. Senate Committee on Banking and Currency (2009), *The Pecora Report: The 1934 Report on the Practices of Stock Exchanges from the Pecora Commission*, CreateSpace Independent Publishing Platform.

Uhlig, Mark (1987), "Jesse Unruh, a California Political Power, Dies," *The New York Times*, www.nytimes.com/1987/08/06/obituaries/jesse-unruh-a-california-political-power-dies.html.

Vaughn, David (2003), "Selected Definitions of 'Hedge Fund'," Comments for the U.S. Securities and Exchange Commission Roundtable on Hedge Funds,' U.S. Securities and Exchange Commission, www.sec.gov/spotlight/hedge funds/hedge-vaughn.htm.

Veasey, E. Norman (1993), "The Emergence of Corporate Governance as a New Legal Discipline," *The Business Lawyer* 48(4).

Ventoruzzo, Marco (2015), "The Disappearing Taboo of Multiple Voting Shares: Regulatory Responses to the Migration of Chrysler-Fiat," *Bocconi Legal Studies Research Paper No. 2574236*, https://ssrn.com/abstract=2574236.

Volacu, Alexandru (2020), "Democracy and Compulsory Voting," *Political Research Quarterly* 473(2): 454–463.

Walker, Owen (2016), *Barbarians in the Boardroom: Activist Investors and the Battle for Control of the World's Most Powerful Companies*, Pearson Education.

Walters, Dan (1988), "War of Succession for California's Bond Empire," *The Wall Street Journal*, March 2.

Winter, Jaap W. (2011), "Shareholder Engagement and Stewardship: The Realities and Illusions of Institutional Share Ownership," https://ssrn.com/abstract=1867564.

Wong, Simon C. Y. (2010), "Why Stewardship Is Proving Elusive for Institutional Investors," *Butterworths Journal of International Banking and Financial Law*, July/August: 406–411. https://papers.ssrn.com/sol3/papers.cfm?abstract_id=1635662.

Acknowledgments

This book is an extension of my collaborative research with William Lazonick on hedge-fund activism, corporations, and economics, which resulted in a book entitled *Predatory Value Extraction* (Oxford University Press 2020). I thank Bill for his continued encouragement and intellectual companionship. I also thank Matt Hopkins for his inputs on hedge funds, and Tom Ferguson and Ken Jacobson for their comments. I am grateful to the National University of Singapore (E-122-00-0004-01), the Laboratory Program for Korean Studies (AKS-2018-LAB-1250001), and the Institute for New Economic Thinking (IN017-00013) for their financial support.

Cambridge Elements

Corporate Governance

Thomas Clarke
UTS Business School, University of Technology Sydney
Thomas Clarke is Professor of Corporate Governance at the UTS Business School of the University of Technology Sydney. His work focuses on the institutional diversity of corporate governance and his most recent book is *International Corporate Governance* (Second Edition 2017). He is interested in questions about the purposes of the corporation, and the convergence of the concerns of corporate governance and corporate sustainability.

About the Series
The series Elements in Corporate Governance focuses on the significant emerging field of corporate governance. Authoritative, lively and compelling analyses include expert surveys of the foundations of the discipline, original insights into controversial debates, frontier developments, and masterclasses on key issues. Its areas of interest include empirical studies of corporate governance in practice, regional institutional diversity, emerging fields, key problems and core theoretical perspectives.

Cambridge Elements ≡

Corporate Governance

Elements in the Series

A full series listing is available at: www.cambridge.org/ECG

Printed in the United States
by Baker & Taylor Publisher Services